D0930865

# Letters to Our Sons

A Mother's Journey—Raising Sons to Become
Men with Character and Courage

YOLANDA CONLEY SHIELDS

iUniverse LLC
Bloomington

Letters to Our Sons
A Mother's Journey—Raising Sons to Become Men with Character and
Courage

Copyright © 2013 by Yolanda Conley Shields.

All rights reserved. No part of this book may be used or reproduced by any means, graphic,
electronic, or mechanical, including photocopying, recording, taping or by any information
storage retrieval system without the written permission of the publisher except in the case of
brief quotations embodied in critical articles and reviews.

iUniverse books may be ordered through booksellers or by contacting:

iUniverse LLC
1663 Liberty Drive
Bloomington, IN 47403
www.iuniverse.com
1-800-Authors (1-800-288-4677)

Because of the dynamic nature of the Internet, any web addresses or links contained in this
book may have changed since publication and may no longer be valid. The views expressed
in this work are solely those of the author and do not necessarily reflect the views of the
publisher, and the publisher hereby disclaims any responsibility for them.

Any people depicted in stock imagery provided by Thinkstock are models, and such images
are being used for illustrative purposes only.
Certain stock imagery © Thinkstock.

ISBN: 978-1-4917-0269-7 (sc)
ISBN: 978-1-4917-0271-0 (hc)
ISBN: 978-1-4917-0270-3 (ebk)

Library of Congress Control Number: 2013915612

Printed in the United States of America

iUniverse rev. date: 09/10/2013

# Contents

# *Acknowledgements*

---

This book would not have been possible without the help of so many of my friends and family. There are numerous colleagues around the country who have aided in conceptualization, publisher selection, and editing. I thank each of you. I'm particularly thankful to all the mothers who participated and believed in this project from the beginning. I am also grateful to my publisher for providing all of the time and support necessary to complete this project. I would like to thank my son, Roland Shields, Jr., for inspiring me to write this book. I thank my mother, Willodes Conley Thompson, for being a great example of a caring and committed mother. Special thanks are extended to Princess Fumi S. Hancock who encouraged and pushed me to finish the book, and E.J. Kerr with E.J. Kerr Designs who prepared the book cover for publication and Deidra Rose who assisted with the editing. Through all the prayers, the Lord truly has blessed this work. My prayer is that it will bless many mothers across the world.

Yolanda Conley Shields

# *Foreword*

Letters are written communication—messages put on paper that provide insight and understanding, with a window to view our history, and instructions for our future. It is important to let your sons know how valuable they are to you and that they have an important role in this world. *Letters To Our Sons* will share the stories of many mothers that are raising sons to become men of character. I join them in writing letters to my three sons and sharing our journey with you.

Dear James D'Wayne II, Jayson Kyle, and Jackson Ron-David,

I was blessed to be born into a big and loving family, with parents that kept Jesus at the center of it all. My father was a strong man. The one significant thing I remember about him was his hands. They were hard, strong, firm, and sure. They were the result of a man who knew no limits to provide and protect his family. My mother was the living example of the virtuous woman in the Bible. She possessed the strength and character that brought glory to her husband and children. She raised me to be virtuous and to wait until the man God would have to be my husband would find me. You know . . . pursue me, court me, do the work of a man to win the heart of a godly woman. Your father was that amazing man, a man I have no regrets giving my life to and together giving life to three wonderful sons.

I am still blessed to have a family of my own, a family of four strapping men that take great care of this here damsel. My prayer is for them to take in the lesson of unity and the power that agreement brings to the unified stand of a family.

As God continues to grace us with the gift of time, I will use it to continue to raise you in the fear and reverence of God the Father and Jesus Christ our Lord. I pray that the three of you will serve God with your life, talent, and treasure and become men of God and men of influence. Stand together as brothers, husbands, and friends. Practice the characteristics of God until they become your own. Be strong, yet kind. Love with all of your heart and hold nothing back. Finally, if you dare to be a fraction of your earthly father, you'll be better than the rest, but, to bear the resemblance of your Heavenly Father, you're guaranteed to be better than the best.

*"Trust in the Lord with all your heart, and do not lean on your own understanding. In all your ways acknowledge him, and he will direct your path."* ~Proverbs 3:5. God's Word has always been the standard by which I live. It was also the standard in which I raised my sons. In God, there is no failure. So, to ensure I didn't fail in rearing the next generation of men, I used the Word of God as instruction and not society. God's Word came with very different views compared to society, but many more promises that I could rely on. God said, "Wide is the gate that leads to destruction, and narrow is the path that leads to eternal life." I chose a different, narrow, unpopular path for raising my three sons. God's Word is the lamp for my feet, and the light for my pathway. I am so proud of my sons, and love them with all my heart.

With much love and faith in my three sons,
Mommy (Debbie Winans Lowe)

# Introduction

**by Olori (Queen) Mary Iyabode Adebayo of
Emure Kingdom, Ekiti state, Nigeria, W. Africa**

*"Motherhood is an embodiment of virtues above price in love,
care, trust, goodness, hard work, help to the poor and needy,
embraced in strength and honor. She is wise and kind."*
                                        ~Proverbs 31:10-31

The foundation for the life of a son is laid with a master plan of a virtuous woman. Imagine the sacrifices of a mother in pregnancy and childcare to adulthood. A good son is basically the product of a good mother.

Every woman desires to have a son, especially in Africa. A son enjoys the special love of both parents and particularly that of the mother who, in African parlance, refers to the son as "husband" and pillar of the home.

A son relates with his mother in the belief that mothers are tender hearted and easily approachable under feminine consideration, unlike the fathers. Mothers are always free with their sons, even in their marital homes, to advise, console, encourage and build hopes for a successful marriage. The spiritual bond started from the womb with a foreseeable future that, when the father is no more, the son represents the interests of the family from generation to generation.

This book is not about mothers raising sons alone, but the role of mothers helping to equip their sons to be men of character. Society expresses the importance of a father and son relationship, but have we really given thought to how vital a mother and son relationship is to our communities and family success? This book will strike a prevailing cord for readers because it's a major issue, especially given that society has always focused on how important a father's role is in his son's life. Has anyone asked, "What's the value of a mother in her son's life?" Think about the cost of a son's success in his everyday connections without his mother's relationship.

In a time of increased violence, drugs, high teenage suicides and pregnancies, our boys are most at risk. More and more are lacking a sense of purpose, struggling at school, awkward in relationships, vulnerable to alcohol and drug abuse, and in danger of being the victims, as well as the perpetrators, of violent crime, physical and sexual abuse. By the age of fifteen, three times as many boys as girls are likely to die from many causes combined—but most especially from accidents, violence and suicide (*Center for Disease Control—CDC*). *So, with this being said, it is crucial that the mothers and fathers play a critical role in the development of sons.*

A mother's role in raising her son is very critical. The father's role is definitely important and needed more and more, but there is something unique about what the mother offers in the raising of her sons since she birthed him. I believe the mother/son relationship will definitely determine how he treats women. Raising boys can be challenging and incredibly rewarding. If you are married or a single parent, there is a tremendous impact that the mother makes on their sons life. As the mother of a son, I know that many mothers have questions, frustrations, and worries specifically related to raising strong, confident young men. As a caring parent, we want to give our boys our very best without enabling them. We want our boys to grow up to be independent, courageous and strong, yet caring and compassionate and to be responsible for themselves, their families and the world. Parents and experts alike agree that raising a son presents its own unique sets of challenges and excitements.

If you're a single mother raising boys, you may be concerned about how to raise a strong young man without a father figure. Or you may wonder how to instill a good work ethic in your son, or worry about how to raise a boy who has a strong sense of his identity and self-worth when he's hanging out with peers and learn to lead and not just follow. Boys who are close to their mothers perform better in school. Mothers often nurture emotional intelligence in their sons, teaching them to recognize and express their own feelings and to be more attuned to the feelings of others. When boys understand this concept, they not only become more articulate, which helps them with reading and writing skills, but also have better self-control in the classroom.

Teenage boys who are close to their moms engage in less risky behavior. It has long been known that good parent-teen communication can help lessen the influence of negative peer pressure. But new research shows that it is a boy's mother who is the most influential when it comes to her son's decision making about alcohol, drugs and sex. Some researchers speculate that the nature of mother-son communication accounts for the difference; mothers usually don't have one big "drug talk" or "sex talk" but instead tend to weave the topic into other conversations or family activities.

I often get asked what I think that boys need the most. I usually hesitate to answer that question because although collectively boys need support in areas such as education and employment, I believe that individual boys have their own needs. However, if there is one thing I believe that all boys need, it is *understanding*. I'm not going to get into a debate about why boys are falling behind girls, but I will shed light on why boys need to be understood. If you do a Google search on boys, you'll find a lot of random stuff, most of it negative. It seems that somehow as we were empowering girls and making sure they succeed in life, we imply to boys that they don't matter. This message permeates throughout our schools and society. We label boys as troubled, angry, aggressive, violent and overall a menace to society. We need to make it clear to boys that they do matter and we need to let them know we care. The best way to get to boys is to show them that we understand.

## At School

Although some parents have the option of homeschooling or single sex classrooms, most parents enroll their sons in schools that have traditional classrooms. Walk into any elementary, middle or high school and more than likely, you'll find a boy either being disruptive or being disciplined. We need to better understand how boys learn and what they need to be engaged at school. We need to understand how to motivate boys to be better writers and readers. We need to understand how it feels to be a boy sitting in a classroom. We need to stop labeling boys and start asking them pertinent questions that will make them more proactive in their learning. Let's give boys more career options and start encouraging them to explore entrepreneurship. Let's offer more interesting classes in middle and high school that will engage boys.

## In the Home

Is your home a learning environment? Do you give your son the freedom to be himself? Let's get past the phrase "Boys will be boys." We need to stop imposing unfair gender roles and characteristics on children, especially boys. Not all boys are rough and tumble. Some boys are quiet and reserved. Let's stop comparing our sons to our neighbor's sons. Let's understand that while boys may need their mothers to nurture and comfort them, they do not need coddling. Let's understand that even if we don't know what it's like to be a boy we can do our best to not work against their natural impulses. Let's stop blaming video games and start being accountable for our son's interest in them, asking why they enjoy them. Let's be more involved in our sons' lives. Let's understand that it is unfair to make insensitive comments to our sons because of our own fears. Let's make the decision to parent based on love, not fear. Let's understand that our misconceptions about boys are causing us to make assumptions about our sons. Let's give our sons the tools they need to be happy, healthy, and successful men. When they are healthy and loved, I believe they become better men, husbands and friends.

## In Society

Let's understand what it means to be a boy and a man in today's society. Let's understand how society views boys and how social pressures cause boys to try to do things that only God can help them accomplish. Let's stop making "bad boys" so appealing in the media. Let's understand that media's portrayal of men depicts to some boys how society views them. Let's understand that what we say about men to boys tells them what we think about them. Let's understand that labeling or making excuses for boys' bad behavior just contributes to the unacceptable behavior. Let's be honest and say as women, we don't know what it feels like to be a boy. Mothers are probably the closest people for all of us, and that's why the role of a mother in raising a son is really huge. It's hard to over-appreciate it!

There is a belief that mothers are always close to their sons and daughters are close to their fathers. Boys learn their earliest lessons about love and trust from their mothers. According to William Pollack, Ph.D., "Far from making boys weaker, the love of a mother can and does actually make boys stronger, emotionally and psychologically." Your son will learn self-respect and confidence when you provide a loving and secure home base for him. When you can create a sense of belonging and significance for your boy, teach him life and character skills, and practice kind, firm discipline, he learns to trust, to face challenges, and to move freely into his world. A strong and loving relationship with a good mother can help a boy learn the skills of intimacy, support him in developing respect for other women, and prepare him for a satisfying relationship someday. Have you prepared your son to become a man of character? Take time to teach and prepare them early, and as they get older, write them a letter that tells and affirms them and gives them permission to be all that they were born to be.

> *"A mother's role in her son's life is important to the success of his future."*
>
> ~Yolanda Conley Shields

**Letters To Our Sons**

Dear Roland, Jr.,

I am so honored to write this letter to you. Scripture says: *"Before I formed you in your mother's womb I knew you; I ordained you a prophet to the nations."* ~Jeremiah 1:5

Roland Bernard Shields, Jr. you were born on October 14, 1991 at Centennial Medical Center in Nashville, Tennessee and started my journey as your mother. This was an exciting time for family and friends. They could not wait for you to come. I knew when you were born that God had a special calling and destiny for you. I remember when you were a baby how I prayed for the Lord to give me great wisdom for raising you. I knew you really were special when you took 24 hours to come into the world. You were not sure if you wanted to come. You have always been a child that loved to talk and make people laugh. You would go to bed talking and wake up talking. I said, "That boy is going to be a lawyer or preacher." I never knew when you were born that I would be a single mom raising you. It was a little scary after the divorce how I would take care of you. I know mothers have a special place in the life of sons, but I also know how important fathers and men are in the lives of young men. I continue to pray for strong godly men to pour into your life. I knew I could never give you what your father should give you.

During our journey together, God has truly blessed us. I know you have seen the great blessings and provision that only God could provide. Even in the hard times, we still trusted God to provide. I remember the times that we would pray for things together and read the Word together. That was very special for me and I will never forget it. Remember, God's timing is perfect.

During your last year of high school, you were so ready for college. You kept asking, "What are you going to do without me?" I asked *you*, "What will *you* do without *me*?" Always remember that you can do anything you put your mind to. You are good in sports, but you are also good with communicating with people. Never underestimate the gifts God has given you. *If* you keep God first and never forget where your provision comes from, He will continue to show you the way.

I know you think I am hard on you, but I just know some of the things you will face out in the world as a young African American male. Know that all the times that I was hard on you, it was definitely out of love for you. You have received the foundation to stand strong in your faith. I pray that you will receive all that your heart desires. I am looking forward to seeing what God has in store for you; not what I want or desire, but what God has for you. His plan is always better than anything we could come up with. So, as you begin your journey as a young man and future leader, there are a couple of things I want you to remember:

- PRAY DAILY
- READ THE WORD
- LOVE THE LORD
- LOVE PEOPLE
- BE A GIVER (TIME, TALENTS AND FINANCES)
- RESPECT YOURSELF AND OTHERS
- BE A MAN OF INTEGRITY

Never

*"For I know the plans I have for you," declares the LORD, "plans to prosper you and not to harm you, plans to give you hope and a future."*

~Jeremiah 29:11 (NIV)

## GET READY FOR YOUR AMAZING JOURNEY!

Love you,
Mom (Yolanda Conley Shields)

# REFLECTIONS

*"A mother's love for her child is like nothing else in the world. It knows no law, no pity; it dares all things and crushes down remorselessly all that stands in its path."*

~Agatha Christie

# Hope for the Next Generation

*"Before I formed you in the womb I knew you, before you were born I set you apart; I appointed you as a prophet to the nations."*

~Jeremiah 1:5 (NIV)

People ask all the time if there is hope for the next generation. It's tough being a boy in America today, but there is still hope. As I look at the statistics for males, especially African American males, it saddens me. I do believe there is hope for the next generation. IF we don't invest time in our sons and let them know that they have a purpose and destiny, they will not have a future. We have been so consumed with work, making money, and ourselves that we have forgotten we are supposed to leave a legacy. Not just the fathers, but mothers as well. Some boys thrive in school. There are more "boy geniuses" than "girl geniuses," and there are more boys in the top one percent of the IQ scale than there are girls. Many boys don't fare as well—and for the majority of them, school may not be as good a fit as it is for girls. "There is no single boy experience at school because there is a wide range of boys—and some take to school and some don't," says Michael Thompson, Ph.D., co-author, *Raising Cain*. "But for the average boy, school is not as good a fit as it is for the average girl. More boys have problems with attention and focus than girls. Because of their higher activity level, boys are likely to get into more trouble than girls. And they are not given enough opportunities to move around—both in

1

actual physical activity and in how they learn—because they spend too much time sitting and not enough time learning by doing, making and building things."

The statistics tell an alarming tale. According to the National Center for Educational Statistics:

- Boys are 30 percent more likely than girls to flunk or drop out of school;

- When it comes to grades and homework, girls outperform boys in elementary, secondary, high school, college, and even graduate school;

- Boys are four to five times more likely than girls to be diagnosed with Attention Deficit Hyperactivity Disorder (ADHD);

- Women outnumber men in higher education with 56 percent of bachelor's degrees and 55 percent of graduate degrees going to women. *According to the U.S. Department of Education:*

- Boys make up two-thirds of the students in special education and are five times more likely to be classified as hyperactive. *According to the U.S. Department of Education*

Parents of boys—stay calm! While the statistics are disturbing, they don't describe every boy—or necessarily your boy—but they do raise concerns about many boys' school experiences. "The odds are that if you come from a family that values education, your boy will be successful in school and will go on to college. Most boys do. However, the average American boy is struggling in school," advises Michael Thompson of *Public Broadcasting Station (PBS)*.

We cannot depend on the school, the church, and community to raise our sons; we have to make sure we are doing our part. It is only hopeless if we give up and not invest the time needed to make a tremendous difference. We need to look at what several young men have been able to accomplish during their young lives. We don't hear enough about it. The media spends more time talking about the negative statistics of young men. Before you go and criticize the younger generation, just remember who raised them. I know that God can protect their hearts and help them to feel loved and cared for even in the midst of the many changes that they experience growing up. Many boys have a hard time expressing their needs to us, especially emotional ones, and we don't want to harm them in any way. There are many things we should do to prepare our sons, such as:

1. Show unconditional love with an emphasis on character and effort more than outcome.

2. Encourage boys to live up to their potential while having reasonable expectations.

3. Love them regardless of whether they make it into Harvard or become a star quarterback.

When my son Roland was just a little boy, I began to pray for God to give him a bright future. I only expected the best for him and was sometimes maybe too hard on him. Being a boy and an only child, I have always felt I had to try and protect him from the cruel things in this world. He has always been very confident and sure of himself. He started his own business when he was just 10 years old. I remember his teacher calling me to let me know that he would not be able to bring his products to school and sell them. I had no idea that he was setting up shop at the school. The students would be waiting on him to see what he had to sell for the day. I knew then that he would have a bright future. He has always been interested in business and how he could make money.

When we see a gift in our children, we have to try and nurture it and help it grow. Your child may not be interested in what you are, but whatever God has gifted them to do, help them to move in that gifting.

I always feared letting him go off to college. As mothers or parents, we sometimes feel they will not make it without us. But many young men have done it for years, so we have to trust that we have imparted great things in them and that they are ready to take on the world; it's good and bad.

During Roland's first year of college, he was attending a gathering at one of the fraternity houses and a shooting took place. A total of 14 students were shot that were standing in the room with Roland. He was the only student who was not shot. I heard about the shooting on the news and immediately called him. When he answered the phone, I knew he was there without him saying a word. I could hear it in his voice. All of my fears that I had about sending him off to college returned. He said, "Mom, I'm okay." I knew he was physically okay, but no one can be mentally okay after something like that. He was lying near the young man that died during the shooting. Even when we see all the negative things that are going on with our sons, I am encouraged when I look at such young people as:

- Jerome Boykin, Jr., owner of JB Sweeping Service in Houma, Louisiana, started his company at the age of 23 after Hurricane Katrina left him jobless.

- Timothy Richard "Tim" Tebow, born August 14, 1987, was a Heisman Trophy-winning American football quarterback for the Florida Gators, as well as quarterback for the Denver Broncos.

- Matthew Charles "Matt" Mullenweg, born January 11, 1984, is an online social media entrepreneur and web developer. He is best known for developing the web software known as WordPress.

- Ephren W. Taylor, II is the youngest African-American CEO of any publicly traded company ever—City Capital Corporation. Taylor started his first business venture at age 12, when he began making video games.

- Amos Winbush, III is a musician who didn't let a Smartphone glitch leave him down and out. Instead, he turned it into a lesson learned—a profitable venture, at that. The CEO of CyberSynchs, a company that allows consumers to sync data between their mobile device and computer, started his multi-million dollar company at the age of 24. He was awarded the Innovator of the Year Award at the 2010 Black Boldness Entrepreneurs Conference.

- Mark Zuckerberg, one of the co-founders of Facebook, became a billionaire at the age of 23. When he showed up in Palo Alto, he had no car, no house, and no job. Today, he's the chairman and CEO of Facebook, and his personal wealth is estimated to be 16.8 billion dollars.

- Alexander Levin, founder and head of ImageShack, created this image sharing site when he was only 17 years old.

- Akil Bello is co-founder and Vice President of Educational Development of Bell Curves, a test-preparation company which he started with his brother at the age of 27.

- Dr. Farrah Gray was named as one of the most influential black men in America by the National Urban League's *Urban Influence Magazine.* At 21 years of age, he was recognized by *Ebony Magazine* as an entrepreneurial icon, business mogul, and best-selling author. He was raised in the impoverished South side of Chicago. Dr. Gray defied the odds and became a self-made millionaire by the age of 14. At the age of 21, he became Dr. Farrah Gray, receiving an Honorary Doctorate degree of Humane Letters from Allen University.

There are many more, but sometimes we only hear about those that are struggling or when they have done something illegal. Don't tell me there is no hope for our sons. Don't just look at statistics; look at what young leaders of this next generation *are accomplishing*. The next generation of young men with character will need:

**Courage**: Courage, also known as bravery, will, and loyalty, is the ability to confront fear, pain and uncertainty.

**Clarity**: Clarity is clearness or lucidity as to perception or understanding; freedom from indistinctness or ambiguity.

**Competence**: Competence is the quality of being competent; adequacy; possession of required skill, knowledge, qualification, or capacity.

**Coachability**: Coachability is the ability to take direction from others.

**Character**: Character is moral or ethical quality: *a man of fine, honorable character;* qualities of honesty, courage, or integrity.

# REFLECTIONS

*"Parents often talk about the younger generation as if they didn't have anything to do with it."*

~Haim Ginott

# REFLECTIONS

*"It is easier to raise boys and girls than to mend men and women."*

~S. Truett Cathey

# REFLECTIONS

*"A mother is someone who can take the place of all others but whose place no one else can take."*

~Unknown

# A Life Well Spent

Raising your sons is not a waste of time but a life well spent. Think back on the time or the day that you were so exhausted after a long day of bathing, tutoring, feeding, reading, or disciplining your son. Even though it was tiring, you woke up the next morning to do it again. The investment pays off years later because of the accomplishments or achievements they have made because of your time invested. I know we sometimes say, "I cannot wait until they are in high school, college or move out." When it gets closer to that time, we begin to worry and want them to be little boys again. If sons or children come from a home background that left them with painful memories, they will find it hard to think kindly toward you. When this happens, many young men grow into bitter men that are not sure how to treat women or people in general. In the hard times of communication with your son, make sure that you are not damaging long-term relationship in order to have things go your way or to be right. Remember not to sweat the small stuff. I am sharing with you things I had to learn over the years.

A life well spent takes patience in the seasons of change for your son. Patience is all about whether you want to get it now or in God's timing. Many of us have been raised without being taught to wait on anything. We live in a microwave society. We want to RIGHT NOW or never.

I look back with gratitude that I have imparted into my son the importance of legacy. He has seen many men in our family do very well and some struggle. He has seen the fruits of both and now understands the importance of making the right decisions. Even when he didn't think my way was cool or out of style, he trusted that I wanted the best for him. He would definitely say the word "cool" is out of style.

As we raise our sons, we need to understand that there will be push back or resistance to our suggestions or decisions. We have to make sure that the decisions we make are not for us, but for the benefit and success of them. We cannot go back and try to live our lives through them. We need to focus on what God has in store for their purpose and destiny. We have to look ahead with faith and know that God wants the best for them. We are to be the teacher helping to guide them into their destiny, not the police demanding that they do what we think is best, even when that doesn't line up with their talents and giftings or what we think they should do. Don't be so hard on yourself if they decide to take a detour and hit some bumps in the road. If you have trained them, they will come back stronger from the experience. Raising your sons is not a waste of time but a *Life Well Spent!*

I asked my son Roland what he remembered about our time together and he said, "I remember spending a lot of time with you being a single mother and me being an only child. I was glad you put me in different activities. I know you did your best and I always knew that you loved me and wanted the best for me. When I was younger, you were somewhat over-protective and that sometimes frustrated me. Being an only child can be hard because there is not another child to be given some of that over-protection. Overall, I had a good life growing up. I am a young man now and the best is yet to come! Thanks for being a great mom to me and the other children you served in the community."

Being a parent is a gift from God and should be a life well spent, not a burden. Can you remember a time when your parents told you how special you were? Didn't it make you feel good? Well, it's the same for your sons. When they think of their mother, you want it to be good thoughts and memories. I'm not saying everything has to be perfect, but there should be good memories that appear before the hard times. My mother disciplined us all, but I still have great memories growing up in my home as a child and love when I am able to go back.

# REFLECTIONS

*"The future destiny of a child is always the work of the mother."*

~Napoleon Bonaparte

# Pointing the Way

---

"*There never was a child so lovely but his mother was glad to get him asleep.*"

~Ralph Waldo Emerson

We want to make sure we always point our children in the right direction, speaking life to them and not negative words. What mothers impart into their sons influences who they become as adult men. I see many men walking around hurt and confused, and when I ask them about their relationship with their mother, I always find heartache or confusion. While guiding them, our motive should be based on their gifts and talents and not what we would desire for them. If they are confident in who they are, and are encouraged in their gifting, they will find their way. I have seen parents push their children to be what they desired and their children end up resenting them.

Faith is also a great part of pointing them in the right way. Mr. Webster defines forecasting as "to predict a future condition or occurrence; to calculate in advance by forethought and foresight in planning." These are not just descriptions and duties of a meteorologist. It's also the responsibility of a parent with their children. Are you accurately assisting your sons in predicting their future by advance planning and careful forethought? Here are six leadership steps to point your son toward God's path for his life.

1. **Help them create tangible goals.** Dare to dream. Habakkuk 2:2 tells us we need more than just a vision; we need to make it plain. In other words, be specific.

2. **Know where you are.** We must evaluate everything, from the needs of our sons, their skills, and even our own thinking.

3. **Know where you've been.** What's your son's history? What has he enjoyed in the past?

4. **Pray for God's plan for them.** Here's what I know: God's plan always works. There is a difference between "Thus sayeth the parent" and "Thus sayeth the Lord!"

5. **Develop the plan.** God doesn't lead us in leaps and jumps; He leads in steps.

6. **Give yourself a test.** Stop and evaluate. Are you assisting or coaching your child to achieve his or her goals?

**Letters To Our Sons**

Dear DeJuan,

I remember when you were conceived and growing inside of me. As a young girl at the age of 17, too young to know anything about being a mother, I took care of you as best I could. I can't say that I made all the right decisions, but how many of us do? Raising you alone was not what I wanted for you, but it's the way things ended up. I prayed that you would be the young man that the Lord formed and ordained while in my womb. I knew as soon as you started to talk that you were a leader—someone who would lead other young boys to be examples to their peers and making sure that the next generation would please the Lord. I remember you trying to be like the other boys in the neighborhood making negative choices and you not really fitting in. The Walmart incident keeps coming to mind. You couldn't do those things and get away with it because you were covered in the blood of the Lord and would be exposed when doing things out of the will of God. I believe the Lord honored this because of my prayer when you were born. Yes, you got several beat downs because I didn't want to have to come to the jailhouse or the cemetery to visit you. I know that you rebelled against a lot of my rules because you thought that I was being strict on you, but it was to mold you into that mighty man of valor that could lead people in the right direction.

In October 1995, our family went through a devastating time with the death of your baby sister, Adriane. I saw you go through some things that were totally against what you stood for, trying to get past what happened. My constant prayers manifested as you later united with a church that would teach you principles of living a life totally and completely for God. In 1997, God blessed us by filling the void of Adriane; a beautiful granddaughter, Raegan, whose mannerisms and personality were just like Adriane's. This change in your life helped you grow up and be the father she needed in her life. We got a kick out of your living arrangements with your 2 friends, you and Raegan. You guys became three men and a baby. Four years later, now married and another child on the way, this will bring another level of maturity in you, prayerfully for another dimension of a life sold out for the Lord. The call on your life is waiting for you to submit to authority and the will of God. Blessings that you have been waiting on will burst from heaven. I am a firm believer that obedience is better than sacrifice.

Love you much,
Mother (Regina Conley Hockett)

# REFLECTIONS

*"A mother is not a person to lean on but a person to make leaning unnecessary."*

~Dorothy Canfield Fisher

**Letters To Our Sons**

Dear Blake, Brady and Brennan,

I am so thankful for each one of you. God gave you as a gift to us years ago, and we have been so grateful ever since. As your mother, you've brought so much joy into my life. I've told people that, "I think I had kids so *I* would grow up!" What I mean by that is, before I had you, my life was care free, and pretty much all about me! When I had you, that all changed, but it has actually made me so much happier, because serving others is what brings joy!

When each of you was born, we dedicated you to God. That, simply put, means that we publicly brought you before the body of believers and chose to say that we were giving the gift God gave us (you!), back to God. Since that time, I have had the realization that you are not really mine . . . you really belong solely to God. He has just allowed your father and me the privilege of raising you. For that reason, I have taken my responsibility to care for you seriously . . . . it's like the parable of the ten talents in the Bible. The Master gave talents to His servants, and upon return, hoped they did something with them instead of relinquishing responsibility for the investment given to them. In the same way, it has been my job to steer you and encourage you to be all you can be in God, as far as your talents and gifts are concerned.

20

Blake, I can remember you as a baby, and even up to now when you're 18 . . . you always had a knack for walking cautiously, thinking clearly, and making great choices. You are truly a man of passion for God, your friends, and your family. You are also a worshipper; both in spirit and in truth, and you lead others into worship through your drumming . . . this blesses me beyond words. All of these attributes are what, I believe, will make you a great husband and father someday. I'm so proud of you!

Brady, the minute you were born, I knew I had a live-wire! I used to say, "Brady is going to go where no man has gone before!" You have a passion to explore the unexplored, to achieve great things, and I hope I've never done anything to stop you! You make everyone around you laugh, which is a BIG gift! Keep dreaming, keep exploring, and keep reaching. Your guitar talent is a gift from God, and you lead people into worship in a talented way . . . I'm so proud of you!

Brennan, you're the youngest, but certainly not the least! You, young man, are such a blessing to this household. God revealed to me when you were only two years old, that you had the gift of wisdom. I have seen that gift of wisdom exercised in almost all you do. You are one who chooses wisely and leads with integrity. I feel honored to be your mother. You have what I call 'sleeping giants' inside of you. You have gifts and abilities not yet realized that will help change the world . . . I'm so proud of you!

I've been asked to write on how my faith has impacted how I have raised you. Well, let's just say, it has been the main source in raising you! I do not know how anyone can raise a child in this world without faith in God. As I've already mentioned, when you were babies, I continually rededicated you to the Lord, realizing you were truly His, and we were simply stewards of what God had given us! In doing so, I found myself always seeking His guidance day in and day out. I've told many other parents who are struggling to raise their kids that, "there's no one book that will give you all the answers . . . just pray for wisdom each day!" And I've done my best to do just that.

As a parent, each new day has the potential to bring on new challenges that we as parents haven't faced . . . so we once again turn to God and ask for His guidance for each day. My advice to you would be to do the same in all areas of your life. God's Word says, "Your Word is a lamp unto my feet and a light unto my path." To me, this has always meant that He gives me just enough wisdom, as I put one foot in front of the other . . . He may not be revealing the path far down the road, but just enough for today. When I pray for you boys, I ask God to guide and direct your steps, that He will protect you always (Psalm 91:9-13), and that you will love Him with all your heart, soul, mind, and strength. I truly believe that if you love God wholly, you will be blessed in all you do. Deuteronomy Chapter 28 lays out a clear path for blessing . . . and it's all about being obedient to God's Word and His commands. My prayer is that you will walk in those blessings, each and every day of your life.

Lots of love,
Mom (Laurie Vilhauer)

# Letting Go And Letting God

Even the wisest mother can find it hard to let go in appropriate ways when her son begins to exercise his independence. Your son desires to do things for himself, from dressing himself to reading his own bedtime story to dating. One of the good and bad things about parenting is that if you do your job as a mother well, your son will eventually leave you. I have spent many days talking with mothers that are in the transition period of sending their sons off to college or on to their own apartment. It can be very hard. I have found myself letting go and then grabbing back to get my son. When I do, I see him pulling back or letting me know that he's okay and asking me to let him grow up. Moms, it will be hard, but you have to let go. You are not only preparing him to be a responsible adult, you are also letting go so he can prepare to be a good husband, dad and friend. If you have poured into them as young children, they will remember what was taught to them, even when you cannot tell or when they are making decisions that you wouldn't make. You want them to be happy about the time they spend with you and not regret it.

*"Train up a child in the way he should go, and when he is old he will not turn from it."* ~Proverbs 22:6. As your son grows, you will learn to find the balance between offering support and stepping back to let him learn from his own experiences—and his own mistakes. Clinging too tightly can create unnecessary power struggles, especially during adolescence (a rather bumpy period for even the closest mothers and sons). Teach skills, listen well and often, have faith in your son, and then let go.

# REFLECTIONS

*"All that I am or ever hope to be, I owe to my angel Mother."*

~Abraham Lincoln

**Letters To Our Sons**

A "Love" Letter to Adebola and Ademola Thompson

Dear Sons,

No words can describe my heartfelt gratitude for God choosing me as a conduit through which you came into existence. Through the years, I have watched you both grow into exemplary young men of God. There are times I wished I could take the credit, but I know better to give the glory to God Almighty Who has and continues to keep you on a path of righteousness.

Adebola and Ademola, in you I see and continue to experience God's grace and His infinite favor. I thank Him for your resilience and your commitment to being all He has called you to be. Against all odds, you have soared through the fiery furnace life has thrown your way and you keep standing. I look at the discouraging stories I hear about teenagers and can't help but thank God for letting me smile where you are concerned. You not only make me smile every time I think about you, you have also brought great joy into my life and the confidence that your steps are indeed ordered by God.

> *"Sometimes our hearts get tangled and our souls a little off-kilter. Friends and family can set us right and help guide us back to the light."*
>
> ~Sera Christann

You show me on a constant basis what true family is about. And I say this prayer—that God Almighty will perfect all that concerns you: that you will never lack for His wisdom to move through life, all that which you lay your hands upon will prosper, and above all, God's immeasurable peace will rule in your lives. Thank you for making me proud. Thank you for not giving up on life when things looked grim. Thank you for always putting a smile on my face every time I thought I could not go on. Today, I only hope I do the same for you.

Your loving mother,
Fumi Stephanie Hancock, RN, Ph.D.

## DEVOTIONAL

> *"It is not flesh and blood but the heart which makes us fathers and sons."*
>
> ~Johann Schiller

My sons Adebola and Ademola were 4 and 2 ½ years old when the divorce finally came through. It was a very difficult time in our lives as I had lost everything I held dear to me and was fighting to hold on to my children. Everything around us looked impossible and the only option which was wide open was to commit suicide. Today, I thank God that He was there through the trials. I mostly thank God that He showed up in the nick of time. Without a solid faith in God, it was practically impossible to raise these young boys, now young men, by myself. I relied on my faith family as the "desert" experience of our lives magnified. My children watched the church family rally around us; they saw faith at work when friends from the church would visit with meals when I could not muster the strength to cook. At the age of 5, Adebola and Ademola began to preach at the church because that was all I ever introduced them to. As a single parent, I knew my children had no chance if I left them to the world's way of doing things. In every decision we made, God was the pivotal Decision Maker. I remember when it was time to relocate from New Jersey to California, we came together as a family (I'm now married to their stepfather, David) and prayed before even considering moving. I continue to teach my children to serve God with all their might and to lean not on their own understanding. More importantly, I show by example.

Today, Adebola is in his second year of college where he is exposed to many "schools of thought" about religion and Christianity. Recently, he shared his thought about religion; how a "one semester" course he had taken had shown him that we did not need Jesus in our lives as long as we were good people and understood that there is a God out there. As a parent, this shook the very core of what I had instilled in him over the years. While

27

Ademola continues to attend church, Adebola is at a crossroads where he is searching for the truth amidst the deceit he has also experienced with "church folks." So, what do you do when you send your child to college to learn and he comes home a different person? I wait patiently and pray earnestly that the God who delivered us during the divorce will magnify Himself in his life and remind him, Adebola, yet again of Who He is—Adebola's Savior.

The lesson learned thus far? As Ademola prepares to join Adebola in college, I will be more involved in his choice of classes. This time, I am also making sure that whichever college Ademola chooses to attend, the importance of attending church services will be engrained in him. Through it all, I rest knowing that the lessons taught to both of my children will rise up in the face of peer pressure and affect a change in their atmosphere. I look forward to when my son, Adebola, finally comes back home to declare that he was right all along—Jesus is Lord!

Recently, we got news of a family member who died on the operating table. This young man loved the Lord with his all of his heart. According to the report we received, he simply went in for a colonoscopy. He came out with a ruptured intestine and when they decided to go back in to re-attach his intestine, he did not make it. This news has shaken the whole family, including my children. Some family members are questioning why God would allow this to happen; others are lifting their voices louder into the sky where our help comes from. With my children, they are learning through life experience that they will not always understand why things happen but they know where to run for help when things look so unbearable. Without being exposed to God at an earlier age, their decision to use this experience as a building block to be closer to God would have been impossible.

Finally, I was indeed moved after discussing the issue of legacy with my children. I needed to know what they thought my legacy would be when I transition. It was positively overwhelming when they both told me that my love for God and my intense servitude are things they will forever take with them and their children. I rest in this knowledge.

> *"You don't choose your family. They are God's gift to you, as you are to them."*
>
> ~Desmond Tutu

# REFLECTIONS

*"When you are a mother, you are never really alone in your thoughts. A mother always has to think twice once for herself and once for her child."*

~Sophia Loren

**Letters To Our Sons**

Dear Vinnie,

Even as I write this letter to you, I smile at the thought of all the names you have: Vincent Rocco Yeackley (named after his 2 grandpas), Vince, Vincey, Vinchinzeo, Vinnie, and Vin. Now seriously, the fact that you have a strong sense of who you are in spite of all the names is a miracle . . . or maybe it's because of all the names and love you've been given! Every year and through every stage of your life your name is changing . . . from the sweetest baby Vinnie, to the now 16, almost 17-year-old young man, Vince.

One story that is still a vivid memory and a picture of who you are happened when you were about eight years old. You were sitting on the fronts steps of our old house in Franklin . . . head in hands . . . so frustrated . . . mad . . . hurt . . . because two of the neighborhood kids who were your friends told you they didn't really believe in God. You said, "How come they don't believe in God? Why can't they believe in Jesus?" That is a true frame of who you are, Vince, and how black and white the world is to you. You are an all or nothing guy. I know this because I am your mother and am wired the same way. I was so proud of you that day! My heart also ached for you knowing how difficult and wonderful life can be when you have such passion in you.

31

I've watched that same little boy pour so much determination and fight into football. You were such a team player and always wanted to be part of something bigger than you. You put all your heart and soul into playing football, and I always held my breath every time you were on the field, not wanting you to get hurt or tackled. (Why did you have to love the roughest sport?) I've watched that young boy become a young man who now pours all that passion and heart and soul into music. Your dad and I raised you on music. You woke up hearing it and fell asleep hearing it. Now that same little boy who went to sleep hearing music is playing late into the night as we fall asleep.

As you have grown more and more into who you are, I've seen God's hand and purpose leading you into your calling as a leader in music and as a leader of men. All we have ever wanted for you, son, was to love God, serve Him, and lead others to Him. The desire and passion that burns in you was put there by the Lord to draw that same passion out of others and help give them purpose, too. To express yourself and be able to create is the way God intentionally created you to be for His glory. You've always been stable and unshakable in your faith. Your tenacity and yes, even your stubbornness, can be your greatest asset in pursuing and meeting all your goals and purpose. All of your giftings are designed to bring others to know Christ, the very thing that eight year old so desperately wanted.

Please forgive me for not being the cooking, baking, craft-making, home-cooked-meal-on-the-table-every-night mom. Forgive me for ever making you feel I was too busy or too tired for you. Please know that I always see you, Vince. I believe in you, Vince— intelligent, creative, funny (except when you're making fun of me), affectionate, sensitive, tender and strong Vince. I will always support you, challenge you, and be your biggest fan. I am for you.

I love you,
Mom (Janna Pastin)

## Mother to Son

*Well, son, I'll tell you:*
*Life for me ain't been no crystal stair.*
*It's had tacks in it,*
*And splinters,*
*And boards torn up,*
*And places with no carpet on the floor—*
*Bare.*
*But all the time*
*I'se been a-climbin' on,*
*And reachin' landin's,*
*And turnin' corners,*
*And sometimes goin' in the dark*
*Where there ain't been no light.*
*So, boy, don't you turn back.*
*Don't you set down on the steps*
*'Cause you finds it's kinder hard.*
*Don't you fall now—*
*For I'se still goin', honey,*
*I'se still climbin',*
*And life for me ain't been no crystal stair.*

~Langston Hughes

**Letters To Our Sons**


Dear David,

> *"You then, my son, be strong in the grace that is in*
> *Christ Jesus. And the things you have heard me say in the*
> *presence of many witnesses entrust to reliable men who*
> *will also be qualified to teach others. Endure hardship*
> *with us like a good soldier of Christ Jesus. No one serving*
> *as a soldier gets involved in civilian affairs—he wants*
> *to please his commanding officer. Similarly, if anyone*
> *competes as an athlete, he does not receive the victor's*
> *crown unless he competes according to the rules. The*
> *hardworking farmer should be the first to receive a share*
> *of the crops. Reflect on what I am saying, for the Lord will*
> *give you insight into all this."*
>
> ~2 Timothy 2: 1-7 (NIV)

This scripture encourages me to be faithful by the grace that I
have in Jesus Christ. I know that I have to be patient, confident
and perseverant in the process of raising you, David. You are only
fifteen and a blessing to us. In this process, I am really comparing
myself to the three people that Paul is talking about. I have been
taught by faithful men and women of God and what I heard, I

really want to teach you, for you to be entrusted and qualified to teach others. When I see how I have to push you to focus, read your Bible, to do your homework, to study your lessons, to remove your plate from the table and so on . . . I really have to continue to be strong and patient.

Like a soldier, whatever fatigue or warfare I can go through to raise you, I will continue to intercede and surrender all to my God and trust Him as a soldier trusts in his commanding officer. Like an athlete, for me to win the victorious crown for you to be a man according to the heart of God, I will always be committed and persevere in prayer for me to see you reflect what I am teaching you. Like a hardworking farmer, I understand that the time for you to become a man of character belongs to God; there will be a season where the precious fruits of my hard work will be rewarded. During the waiting time, discouragement, lack of patience, doubts and questions are on my way. In life, when the soldier thinks about the victory, the athlete about the crown, and the farmer about the harvest, they always recover their strength and have hope, courage and confidence. As I see you growing, I have hope in Christ that you will become that man of character that God is looking for. As a mom, when I feel discouraged, I always go in your room to pray and declare all the promises that the Lord has for you in the Bible.

Your Mom (Rose Lusangi Phambu—France, Congo, USA)

# REFLECTIONS

*"Mothers hold their childrens' hands for a short while, but their hearts forever."*

~Anonymous

**Letters To Our Sons**

My Dearest Adam,

I am writing you this letter in hopes of sharing with you information about your past, insights into your present, and in general, my heart for you. I want to share with you not only hopes and dreams, but life and love lessons I have learned. I pray they inspire you and I hope they will help you in your walk through life . . . and if I have done my job well, you'll be sharing some of these life lessons in a letter to your children.

I can't tell you what a privilege it is being your mom and how happy I am that God chose me for you! These ten years have flown by. I remember the day I found out I was pregnant with you. I did not know it immediately. I'll never forget when the nurse was giving me my regular examination. She brought out the ultra-sound, stood in front of the screen, and proceeded to take a picture of you in my womb. You were only ten weeks old, but I knew God had ordained you to enter into my life at "that" particular time. You see, your grandfather had passed away just a few months earlier after losing his battle with Alzheimer's and diabetic complications. You and he share the same middle name of Edward, as well as, the love and curiosity of science, aviation, and engineering. I knew in the womb you were a boy; I knew then you were going to be a "special" young man.

Most women considered my pregnancy with you a "dream." I had none of the signs and symptoms common in most pregnancies. I worked out every day, including the day you were born (which occurred in a record breaking 45 minutes). I swam a lot while pregnant. I am sure I am single-handedly responsible for your active disposition and your love for the water! In spite of the stressful circumstances that surrounded the nine months preceding your birth, (the death of my father, 9/11, the loss of my job, financial challenges and marital trials), I was determined your time in the womb would be tranquil. Through it all, God was not only faithful, He provided . . . and provided in abundance. I can still see His hand and His favor on your life.

You accepted Jesus on the drive to school. You just turned five. I was listening to a Christian radio station when a commercial came on and asked if you knew Jesus, and further stated that if you wanted to be with your loved ones again, you would have to accept Christ. You said, "Mommy, I want to know Jesus because I want to see you again in heaven." I could hardly fight back the tears as I led you in a prayer accepting Christ as your Lord . . . and you have been running with Jesus ever since.

I am amazed by your tender heart, your resilience . . . your constant ability to rise above each and every circumstance. You have an uncanny ability to love. You choose to see the best in people. I will never forget a special day in first grade at Christ Presbyterian Academy. One of your classmates was crying because she missed being at home. You ran and put your arm around her and told her not to cry. "It's going to be alright," you said. And again, whether on the playground or the soccer field, you seemed to be the first person to assist an injured teammate. When Mario was swimming in his first swim meet, and he began to cry, you placed your arm around his shoulder and said, "I remember what it felt like my first swim meet. I was nervous, too. But you are going to do just fine." Adam, one of my prayers for you is that you keep this tender heart. I hope you always strive to show grace and love in all situations. I realize I cannot protect you from the pain or mistakes which can come from possessing a tender heart. But without these, how can we ever hope to grow? So, my love, it is best to learn quickly from mistakes and never live life in fear of making them . . . and definitely don't make the same mistake twice!

My son, learn to value the beauty of "right" friendships. Remember, there are those that add to your life, and those that subtract and divide. Don't waste your valuable, precious time with relationships that leave you drained or feed qualities and characteristics of a young man you do not want to become. Make sure that those that have been in your presence can say of you, "He has been a good friend."

Grow to be a man of your word. In this life, your word is really all you have at the end of the day. Do what you say you will do. If people cannot believe what you say, or in what you say, what can they believe about you? Use your words wisely. Use them to build up, not tear down. But if you must tear down, make sure it is using the Word of God to speak to mountains, pull down strongholds, build up faith and praise the Lord!

Always keep the love of learning! Never grow tired of it. Knowledge is a gift gained through experience and exposure. Make sure you open it each day!! My beloved son, live your life fully. Choose to find the beauty in all things. Learn the beauty of giving as a part of living. Be patient with love. Don't settle for something God did not give you. But when you find it, guard it, nurture it, and grow in it together. Value "couple-ship" over personal agenda. Honor and respect each other above all. Live and love with the knowledge you are leaving a legacy. Above all, know that I love you more than there are stars in the sky. You are the best part of everything I am and everything I hope to be. You are my legacy. Thank you for the privilege of parenting you.

Love,
Mommy (Carolyn Foster)

**Letters To Our Sons**

Dear Sons,

Being a mother of three sons is somewhat paradoxical. I see you all through what I am praying for you to be since you were born. I see that growing from a seed, to a tender plant, to a blooming, stable plant, to a maturing plant. As with any new, young plant like a tomato plant, you place a stick or pole next to it for support to keep it stable. I feel like that's my job to do since your dad passed away. I am that post to stand beside you. I know that this will change and may end someday. I don't want it to end and no one may give you credit . . . that you are there. On the other hand, I do not want to emasculate you as men . . . My desire is that you grow and mature as strong men, as black men to follow in the heritage of your father, grandfathers and uncles. I hope that you will be strong but in touch with your emotions to shed a tear, which is the underlying strength, and to be balanced. Now that James is gone, I don't feel that I am stepping into his shoes. I am unable to fill his shoes because he had pretty BIG shoes and I cannot even try spiritually or emotionally to do what he was able to do.

I want you to go forward into your God-given talents and gifts and to be salt and light in the marketplace. I know that you will have struggles in this life, but don't be desperate; the world and our enemy, Satan, are waiting for you to feel that desperation and make unwise/poor decisions. I pray that you will cry out to God for wisdom in your life choices. I hope that you will embrace a time of intimacy with GOD to hear and discern His voice above all the chatter of the current social media. Sometimes I feel that I'm in a battle with Satan over you, but that is in the mind and that is the battlefield. The battle belongs to God and as you trust Him, you will have the victory! Don't forget to surround yourself with godly men that will encourage you with a word of wisdom, not only to tell you "MAN UP," but encourage you to open your heart so that you can hear and receive wise counsel for your lives. The Word of God says that He will be the Defender of the widows and orphans and He will be a Father to the fatherless . . . That's what I declare!

Love you,
Mother (Carol Harris)

## Devotional—Thank Jesus for Every Circumstance

*"Give thanks in all circumstances; for this is the will of God in Christ Jesus for you."*

~1 Thessalonians 5:18

We sometimes treat God like an ATM. When we come to God in prayer, we need to come not expecting anything but thanking Him for all things. So, throw your list away and just come with an open heart because He already knows what we need before we ASK. Make it a habit of coming into a time of prayer when you have nothing to ask for. Come first into His presence with praise and worship and with no agendas. He is the King of Kings and Lord of Lords and He cares about you! He is able to redeem every situation and convert what is troubling into something positive. He asks me to trust Him and to give thanks in every circumstance. He is able to make our prayers less about us, more about others, and it will deepen our prayer life and bless the time we spend with Him.

Faith Step: Organize your prayer with intention today. Praise Him first. Thank Him second. Confess. Then bring your request to Him.

**Letters To Our Sons**

Dear Christopher,

I remember so clearly the day you were born. On that day, April 3, 1995, my whole world changed. Everything I had planned changed, and everything I thought I knew became irrelevant. I felt as though I had been handed a new beginning when they handed me the 7-pound, 11-ounce miracle I named Christopher. I picked the name Christopher because it means "carrier of Christ" and I wanted to implant that purpose in you from the beginning. You were so beautiful and so brand new that I couldn't help but to think that, for you, I had to do better and be better than I'd ever been before.

Since I had you by cesarean section, they did not allow you to stay with me for long because I was recovering from the drugs they had given me to numb my belly. But, it was not long before I realized how undeniable the connection was that God had given us. It was around 1 a.m., just 3 short hours after you had arrived, that I felt an aching in my breast. It was not a painful ache; I felt it and knew it was there. I sat straight up in my bed with a feeling of anticipation and expectation—for what, I did not know. I looked around the dark room and tried to figure out why I was sitting there and what exactly I was waiting for when suddenly my hospital room door swung open. The nurse that appeared in the doorway seemed a little surprised to see me sitting up and asked if I felt okay. When I told her I was fine, she said, "Good, because there is a hungry little guy that wants to see you." The nurse went on to explain that you woke up crying to be fed right around the time I'd sat up in the bed. That is when I realized what maternal instincts were. As the nurse helped you latch on to be nursed for the first time, my eyes filled with tears as your natural instinct to nurse kicked in and my natural instinct to feed you and protect you took over my very being. From that moment in time, my ministry as your mother began.

In you, God gave me a gift, but He has also charged me with nurturing the purpose that He has placed in you until you come of age. That is a huge responsibility and one that I do not take lightly. However, I also know that once you become a man, that purpose then becomes your responsibility. In the meantime, I am responsible for fertilizing, watering, and pruning the seeds of destiny God has planted in your belly. From the time you were born until now, I have always been mindful of your manhood. The Word tells me to "Raise up a child in the way that he should go and he will not depart." This is my part, and for me, that has always meant that I had to make a conscious and intentional effort to help you discover "your way." See, God gives us all a way, but it is not the same for everybody. Your "way" may not be someone else's way, and vice versa. The "way" that God refers to is your purpose, and as a mother, I cannot raise you up in the way you should go unless I help you to discover your purpose. Once it is discovered, then you must nurture it.

I have always tried my best to surround you with people and experiences that would help you find your way to manhood. Your grandfather has always been a wonderful example for you, and I thank God for allowing him to be part of your life since the beginning. From the time we moved back to Tennessee from Maryland (when you were only a few months old), you have been the apple of his eye. He taught you how to throw a ball, drive the riding lawn mower, and how to ride a bike before you went to kindergarten; and your cousin Mike taught you how to pee standing up!

I was determined to do my part to contribute to your "man lessons" so I put you in Tae-Kwon-Do classes when you were six to help you learn self-discipline. I signed you up to play basketball and baseball to give you time with positive male role models. I've enrolled you in a number of mentoring programs to help you academically and socially, and I have seen you benefit from all of those experiences. I used to be offended when I would hear people comment that a woman could not raise a boy to be a man. I thought it was a sexist and narrow-minded opinion. After all, since your father was not around, what choice did I have but to raise you myself and teach you everything I knew about being a man? How foolish was I! Slowly, I started to realize over the years that I was not equipped— physically, emotionally or mentally—to teach you how to be a man. I gradually came to the realization of my limitations in this area, but there was one morning in particular when it really hit home.

You were twelve years old and we were getting ready for church. On that Saturday, you reminded me that you were supposed to wear a tie to church the next day. So, I went and purchased a tie for you—a real tie, not a clip-on. So, that Sunday morning while we were getting dressed, you came to me and asked for my help in tying your tie. At first, I felt confident that I'd remember how to tie a tie . . . after all, I'd worn ties in the 80's when it was in fashion. As a child myself, I'd seen your grandpa tie his tie for years as he dressed for work. After several attempts, I realized that I could not remember how to tie a tie! I remained calm and got your grandpa on the phone for some over-the-phone instructions. Needless to say, between your frustration with me, my frustration with the tie, and Grandpa's frustration with both of us, I couldn't figure it out. I logged on to YouTube, found some video instructions, and we were eventually able to get a decent looking knot before it was time to go to church that morning. You probably remember this incident as well as I do, but what you don't know is that at one point that morning, I went in the bathroom and cried like a baby. I felt that I had failed you. I felt that I had let you down. I felt like I was the cause of you failing one of the most basic lessons of manhood.

That day, I realized that although I was charged with the responsibility of making sure you are "trained up in the way you should go," I cannot be the only teacher. There are lessons that you must learn from other people in other ways. So, I decided the wisest thing to do would be to create a network of men that have your best interest at heart. They are ministers, coaches, teachers, relatives, church members and friends that love you and want the best for you. The people in your network know your dreams and your goals, and they know your challenges. Some of them hear all of the things that you don't want to share with me, and some of them probably know some things about you that I don't know yet, but that's okay.

By far the most important gift I have given you is God. My ministry is praying for you and helping you learn to live a life that is pleasing to God. My goal is to help you discover the purpose that God has placed in you and how to turn that in to your own ministry. I am determined to meet that goal. It has not always been easy, and Lord knows that I have stumbled along the way, but rest assured that everything I have ever done has been with your best interest at heart. One of the scriptures that God has given me to share with you is Proverbs 24:27. You hear me say it to you so much that you should know it by heart! It says, *"Complete your outdoor work, and prepare your field; afterwards, build your house."* (CSB) This scripture is the key to you becoming a man. It tells you to do the work, be prepared and once you have laid a foundation, build your house. Your house is your career, your family, and your ministry. You have big dreams and I believe in them all, but always remember that there is a distinct difference between dreaming and living your dreams. One you can do while you are sleeping or resting; the other you can only do with your eyes wide open. I always remind you that with God all things are possible because eyes haven't seen and ears have not heard the things that God has prepared for you, because you have been called according to His purpose. You are my son, but you are His child. Being a single mother is not easy, but God has always been my ever-present help. Because of Him, we have never been homeless or hungry. Because of Him, we have always been able to be together under the same roof. Because of Him, we both have purpose and destiny that cannot be denied. The world does not want to see you succeed at fulfilling the purpose God has given you, but if you learn to lean and depend on God in all that you do, there is nothing the world can do to stop you.

Statistics say that black boys raised by single mothers have a higher chance of going to jail than they do of going to college, but God says you are more than a conqueror. The world looks at you and says what you cannot be, but God says that you are the righteousness of Christ and that you were created in His image. So, build your house, son. Build it on good ground with a strong foundation of faith. Build it with hard work and determination. Build your house with love and peace and joy in your heart. My faith in God has allowed me to be a good mother. Yes, I've given myself permission to say, "I am a good mother." No, I am not a perfect mother. Yes, I've made mistakes, but God has given me a roadmap in the form of the Holy Bible. He has cleared paths for my son to be in the right place at the right time, so many times. I depend on Him for answers when my son asks questions that I don't understand. If it was not for my faith in God, I would not be able to let him walk out of the door each day with confidence that God will watch over him. Because of my faith, I am able to tell my son to build his house and I am confident that he can. I tell him that with God, he can reach any goal and any dream that God has placed in him. I truly believe that and it is my purpose that my son knows it, too.

Love,
Mom (Brigette Brandon)

# REFLECTIONS

*"Life is not measured by the number of breaths we take, but by the moments that take our breath away."*

~Maya Angelou

**Letters To Our Sons**

Dear Sons,

This letter is written to my three sons; John Fard (24), Gershom Hakim (21), and Elijah Rahim (19). The journey of being a single parent began very unexpectedly. No one could have told me that your father and I wouldn't complete the journey together. We were very much in love, and as a result of our love, we had you and your sister Nia. Wow, what wonderful gifts of love you are and have been. I am going to keep this real and be very honest. Being a single parent was never something I wanted; it was forced onto me because of choices your father made and choices I had to make. Being a single mother was difficult, overwhelming, and faith-producing, but just like the songwriter wrote: 'I wouldn't give anything for my journey.' Fard, (Nia), Gershom and Elijah—as hard as things got and as tight as things are, you all have made this life, my life, worth living. Don't get me wrong; there are others who make my life wonderful—God, siblings, friends, the children I teach and their families—but you all are at the top of my list (God first) of what I love and live for.

I've been asked to write about my journey as a single mother raising boys, and man, is that difficult! It's difficult because I want to rush ahead and tell you how the journey turns out. I want to write about how, at the end of the journey, we win! I want you to know that it's true; everything the Bible said is true! I want to rush ahead and tell you that you become and do everything God has planned for you to become and do.

Fard, I want to rush ahead and let you know that your Daddy's got you!! First and foremost, your father loved you; he did the best he could with what he had, or so he thought he had. You were his first born, the pride of his heart. Any pain and hurt you experience because your father isn't there . . . you have to let it go! You have to forgive him. Remember, he was only a man, and the Bible tells us that man will fail us, but by His very nature, God will never fail you. I know it seems like you run into brick walls at every turn. I know you are struggling to go to school, find work and support your family; you're on the right track! Stay focused on your goals and keep in mind the big picture! Remember the choices you make today can be a stepping stone or stumbling block to your future. You're not an island and you don't stand alone, although sometimes it may seem like it. God has blessed you with natural abilities to think deeply and retain information. Don't let the enemy tell you lies about yourself. I told you years ago, and will continue to tell you, that God has a special calling on your life and the devil is going to try to do all he can to distract you—don't fall for it. The enemy is an optical illusionist, he will try to make things seem like they are, but they really aren't. God has given you the power and the authority over all of the enemy's tricks, traps and lies. Cast him out and don't allow him to return to your situation. Fard, here's the deal—you are my son and you weren't made to break, and there's nothing you can do about it.

As for you, Gershom, I want to rush ahead and tell you how all your hard work and determination paid off. I know you had many disappointments, but God is not man that He can lie. By definition alone God can do everything BUT fail. All of the promises He made you are YES and AMEN! Get in agreement with Him. You aren't just a blessing to your family, but you are a blessing to the world. As big as you are (6'6" and 285 pounds) you are a gentle, peaceful spirit. People who know you know the truth in this. God has blessed you with His peace and great strength. You will have opportunities to represent God in word and action in the world. As a child, you wanted to become a professional athlete and represent God; you will do it because God has anointed your life to influence the world for Him. God has a plan and a purpose mapped out for you and the more you seek Him, the clearer His will for your life will be.

Elijah, although you are the youngest of the family, you seemed to have grown up the quickest. Don't get it twisted; you still have a ton of growing to do. Going to school away from home (2 years Ohio, 1 year Georgia, and now Southern University at Shreveport, Louisiana) has taught you things you wouldn't have learned at home from me. Actually, one of the reasons I allowed you to go to school in Ohio was because I wanted to make sure you had some strong, positive, black men in your life. If I could, I would rush ahead and tell you that you get those degrees . . . that you will reach back into communities to motivate and encourage high school students, especially freshmen, on the importance of getting those grades on the front end of their education as opposed to waiting until their senior year. I want to rush to the part of the journey where you have learned to cast all of your cares on God because He cares for you. You are extremely goal oriented; sometimes you get so focused on the goal that you jeopardize it by not wanting to go through the process. Man plans, but God is the best of planners. Remember, you win, you make it, and you attain it. Just don't make it harder on yourself than it has to be. We see your swagger . . . go on and walk it out because you walk in the favor of God.

I want to rush to the part of my journey that lets other single parents know that God's got them and He is the only thing that will sustain them through this process. Remember, that's all it is—a process—a process of becoming what God desires of us. Like

I said before, I didn't choose this journey directly, but indirectly by some of the choices I made, I did chose this journey. I like to believe I chose the wrong journey, but as God said in His Word, He will turn what the enemy meant for bad to good.

When your father and I married, I thought it would be forever. As much as I tried, I can't blame your father for everything. There were things I could have done differently, but ultimately he made the final choice to dissolve the marriage. He also made the final decision on what his relationship would be to you all. I've always encouraged you to love and respect your father. I tried to get you to understand that he had things going on in his life that caused him to act the way he did, but he was still your father and loved you the best he could.

Divorce can be painful for everyone involved and I thank God for His peace and joy. I thank God for healing. Long before I ever knew it, I was being prepared for the role of single motherhood. One evening, I wanted to go to the store and buy food for dinner. I didn't have any money nor did I have a car. I told your dad what I wanted to do and he told me to wait. I waited. I waited for him to relax, take a shower and talk to a friend. In the meantime, my children were hungry and it was getting late. That is when I realized I was totally depended on him. I had no family in Nashville, I didn't have any money, and I didn't have a car. I thought to myself—what would happen to me and my four children if this man up and left us or even died? How would I get around? How would I feed my children? How would I pay bills? The next couple of days, I got busy and found a job. When your father and I separated (actually before), I didn't allow myself to sit down and think about what I was doing or how I was going to do it; I just did it! I was raising four children, going to school full-time, and working full-time. It was the grace of God that allowed me to do all that. So, here I am today with three degrees and a couple of teaching certificates—never lost a child or a job in the process! As a matter of fact, all of you have either finished college or are degree-seeking students now. Because of God's grace and mercy, I own my own home, car, and have a career I love! It hasn't always been like this—but God!!!!

Let me share a few life-changing moments in my struggle to be a good mother and contributing member to society. I remember when we used to live in what people call the 'projects.' We were on welfare and received food stamps, but I remember the day I went through the whole (what I saw as degrading) process to re-apply for assistance and they told me my gross was $5.00 over the limit. I was relieved and scared. I wasn't sure how I was going to feed you all, yet I was glad I didn't ever have to 'beg' again. I will say that I thank God for the help, because I needed it, but I am extremely pleased that I didn't become dependent on the system. I became dependent on God!!!!!

I remember the day one of my instructors at T.S.U. (Dr. Leslie Drummond) took me into her office, shared scripture with me, and told me that I needed to find a place of worship, a place where I could hear the truth about God, a place where I could find peace. You see, she saw beyond the mask I was wearing. I was deeply depressed and overwhelmed. Dr. Drummond saw that I was heading to a place (mentally) that could be destructive to us all. Again, it was the grace of God that led us to Born Again Church.

I remember the nights/days I would cry because I couldn't give you all the simple things that other children had. A co-worker once saw Nia dressed in a cute little dress with matching stockings and told me, "I know if you could afford it, you really would dress your children cute." I am not certain what she meant, but I was so hurt to know that my best still wasn't good enough. I remember the time a close friend gave us some hot dogs that were left over from a church event, and as she brought them into the house, you said, jokingly (I knew and you knew what you meant when you all said), "When I grow up, I will never eat another hot dog!" Maybe that's why Elijah is a vegetarian.

I remember I was going through what seemed like hell; separation, loss of my mother, little to no money, and feeling very alone and isolated. I was working at Head Start and we were having a celebration. This lady sang a song that spoke of God, teaching her to depend on Him. She sang that she knew her friends and relatives would be there for her, but God was teaching her to depend on Him. God ministered to me right there in that room. It's been over fifteen years and I haven't been able to forget the impact that song had on me. I realized right then and there that God was at work teaching me to depend on Him and Him alone.

I remember standing on the balcony of our apartment as the sun was going down, crying because I missed my mother so much, and not understanding why I was in Nashville, Tennessee where I had no family and very few friends. Deep inside of me, I knew God would never leave me. I remember the time I was ready to give up. I didn't want to live any more. I was okay with my sisters taking care of you all. We were getting ready for church and I remember the pain and grief I was feeling. I was trying to get you all dressed for church myself and it seemed like things kept going wrong; stockings running, kids running around, hair wouldn't do right . . . but 'something' made me press on. When I got to church and the altar appeal went forth, it was God's grace that moved your Aunt Susie to ask me if I wanted to go to the altar. I went and there was a warm feeling that moved across my body and peace swept over me that hasn't left me since. It was the peace and joy that comes only from God. I was still weeping, but I was smiling at the same time.

I am sharing all of this to let you know that although we still struggle financially and there are things that I am not able to give you, I thank God that not one day did you go to bed hungry. Not one day did we ever sit in the dark or not have water or heat because I didn't money to pay a bill. Not one day did we have to beg for anything. Let me take it one step further—between full scholarships and financial aid, I never had to pay out of my pocket for your education (not counting summer school). Why? Because God's got us!!! We walk in favor! We are blessed and highly favored! I trust God because I know that I know who He is and I know who I am/we are in Him. The only thing about this letter is that it's my journey. God has a journey for each of you and the only thing you need on this journey is a personal relationship with Him. Try God for yourself and watch what He does! I love you with love that only God can give me as 'your' mother.

Love,
Mom (Patricia Klutz)

# REFLECTIONS

*"I remember my mother's prayers, and they have always followed me. They clung to me all my life."*

~Abraham Lincoln

# MOTHER AND SON

My son
I am here
I cannot protect you
From the world.
My son
I am here
I can only love you
No matter what.
My son
I am here
My love unconditional
On this you can rely.
My son
I am here
To guide and to teach you
And now you must fly.
My son
I am here
Life can be difficult
I hear your cry.
My son
I am here
Changes are painful
Never forget who you are.
My son
I am here
Maintain the faith
In yourself and in God.
My son
I am here
Self-acceptance is yours
Do not fear.
My son
I am here.

-Author Unknown

# REFLECTIONS

*"Men are what their mothers made them."*

~Ralph Waldo Emerson

## To My Son

Oh, how the years go by,
Time has surely flown by.
I still have hopes and dreams for you, that
You will accomplish all that your heart desires.
Allow God to lead and guide you
And you will never go wrong.
Your laughter and smile
Bring me joy and lets me know
That you are on the right path.
Never forget to pay it forward
Since you have been given much.
Remember that no one can stop
What God has ordained for you!
Walk in your destiny daily.
I am your biggest cheerleader
And will always love you.

~Yolanda Conley Shields

# REFLECTIONS

*"A mother understands what a child doesn't say."*
~Jewish Proverb

**Letters To Our Sons**

Dear Donovan,

Oh, how God knew that I needed a mild-tempered baby. You were born shortly after surviving the tragedy of losing your Aunt Beverly to domestic violence. Most mornings, I would wake up to see you lying in your crib smiling, patiently waiting for me to get up. You rarely cried, which made the extreme transition in our home manageable. You see, I was expecting my first baby (you), but by the time you were born, your cousins, ages five and ten, had come to live with us due to the death of their mother. Your half-sister Nikki also came to live with us shortly before you were born.

Growing up, you were amazingly obedient, loving, and tenderhearted. You have always been sensitive to sin and expressed sadness for hurting God when you disobeyed. As you transitioned from boy to young man, the enemy has tried to steal what has been planted in your heart and does not want you to live a powerful and effective life for God. I know that many times you wish I would be content with just having a good son. I mean, compared to the world's standards, you are a model teenager. My goal for you, though, is to be a mighty man of God. Valor, honor, and respect are the virtues that I desire for you. God wants you to be a leader for His people, standing in the gap as a warrior for many who are in need of God and are crying for help. You are called to be a man after God's own heart and a servant who is willing to get his hands dirty in this mixed up world. You see, my standard for you is God's standard. In His Word, He has promised that you can be everything that He has called you to be. There are so many boys younger than you that are crying out for an example, for someone who will be real and say, "Hey, I know I am going to make mistakes, but you can follow me as I strive to follow Christ."

God has His mighty hand on your life. When the spirit of pornography tried to rear its ugly head in our home through the Internet, God had your back. When the sexting tried to enter through the cell phone, God had your back. Every time Satan has tried to surface in music or any avenue, God has revealed him for who he is. Never look at it as "I got caught," but as the enemy being exposed. God will expose the enemy every time to protect those that He is preparing to be a soldier in His kingdom. You see, my son, a soldier cannot get caught up in civilian affairs. And the Lord chastens those He loves. I know you are thinking, "Mom, why are you telling my business?" I am not telling your business. Trust me; there is not a teenage boy or man that has not been tempted in the same way. Your goal is to prevent someone else from falling into Satan's trap, even though they *will be* tempted. It is not the temptation that is evil, only if you act upon it does it become evil. So, my prayer for you is that you will allow no one to despise your youth, but you are an example in life, love, speech, and action no matter what your friends choose to do. You have been a great encouragement to me. You seem to know when I am discouraged about something without me telling you. What a blessing to have a son who is sensitive to what is going on with his mom! I am so grateful to have a son like you. You have been a joy to raise and I am looking forward to seeing what God has in store for your life.

Love,
Mom (Shelia Patterson)

## DEVOTIONAL

> *"I can do all things through Christ who strengthens me."*
> ~Philippians 4:13 (NKJV)

I never had a son, but I remember when my first grandson was born, I prayed that he would never be a statistic. Out of that prayer came a quote that I typed out and read to him daily. At the age of two, he was saying it back to me. "I will not be a statistic. I have the mind of Christ and a spirit of excellence; therefore, I choose to walk in that excellence daily." Today he is seventeen and I still have him quote it from time to time.

~Deronda Lewis

# REFLECTIONS

*"Mothers have as powerful an influence over the welfare of future generations as all other earthly causes combined."*

~ John S.C. Abbott

**Letters To Our Sons**

Dear Pappy (Ron),

You know that I love you, no matter what you do. I don't like nor understand some things you have done, but I still love you. I want to tell you so much, but my thoughts and words are not working together. I have often told you how proud I am of the way you and God have turned your life around.

Saturday, November 27, 1982 at 10:17pm—I will always remember—that was the day the Lord blessed your father, Vanal, Sr., and I with you. My delivery was fast with few pains, not at all what I had been told. I heard you cry; the doctor said, "It's a healthy boy," and I started crying. I asked if you had all fingers and toes, a head full of black curls and cute little lips, and what was that bald spot in front of your forehead, a birth mark? Oh, you were absolutely the sweetest thing I had ever seen! I can't explain the feeling that came over me; the joy of knowing that you were mine, after years of trying to conceive and now, I am holding you. WOW!

Ron, you had some sickness during the first year; asthma, colic, a lot of rocking and walking to quiet you. Were you spoiled? Well, let's say that you were much loved. I made up a song just for you called "Mama's Little Love." It was all out of tune, but it stopped the crying (maybe so I would stop singing!).

Marital problems started when you were about eighteen months old, although you never knew it. One thing led to another; without going into detail, things were not good. Our relationship went from bad to worse, mostly money problems, but I was determined that you would not be affected. We divorced, and you and I moved from our nice brick home into a very comfortable apartment across town. We were starting all over again, but I remember that you said we were a team. I will never forget that my son wanted to be my team member! Thank God for the people He put in our life to help us along our journey! Vanal's mother, Grandmama Colleen, always took care of us, encouraged me, and she prayed for us. I will never forget her.

Well, as the story goes, we settled into our daily routine. You were in elementary school at Park View Christian and I was working 12-hour shifts as a nurse at Park View Hospital. Before and after school care, karate classes, football practice, and homework; we stayed very busy. You know how much your father helped us . . . not at all, in any way, visits or money! Moving right along . . . some things are best left buried.

As we were getting used to being our own team, God had another plan for us. A good-looking man entered our life . . . a preacher, pastor, and much older man I only knew as Fred Eugene Conley. A lot of drama that you don't even know about happened before I started dating him. If you must know, ask, and I will tell you. I fell madly in love with Fred, and he with me. So many people were against the idea. It was a dark time in my life that I hate to mention. I prayed for guidance about whether I needed this old pastor with so much baggage in my life. I didn't know how to be a pastor's wife, and I wasn't sure that I wanted to. You loved him and thought we should give it try. Fred convinced me that we three needed to be together and asked me to marry him. I said yes. Fred gave us hope, taught us so much, and loved me and you as if you were his own. Well, Vanal wasn't crazy about the marriage either, but had never done anything for you, so his vote didn't count. You were thrilled about the engagement and told all your friends that you and I were getting married; not your mother, but *we* were getting married.

Fred was good with you. As you got older, Fred taught you how to take care of yourself, about girls, how to drive, and most of all, how to be a real man. He taught mainly by setting examples. I know that you learned so much from him. Not only did we get a great man, I also got some daughters and you, some sisters. A total package!

Ron, I know there were many things you didn't want to do like singing in the choir at church, serving on the usher board, and being in plays, just to name a few. But Fred's rules were "you live in this house; you abide by our rules." But, look at you now! Aren't you glad that you got late night talks and the whippings?

In 2004, Fred was diagnosed with lung cancer and died October 25, 2005 . . . 3 days after my birthday. I thought it was the end for me. What pain, what disappointment from God! I was so sure that God was going to heal him on this side. Yes, I was mad at Him. I had shouting matches with God, crying spells, experienced weight loss . . . everything. Fred did everything for me.

You moved out with that Asian girl that we didn't approve of. I was so caught up in my own grief that I didn't see what you were going through. That's when you moved back home, started staying out, using alcohol, cigarettes, skipping your classes, lying, and other things you shouldn't have been doing. What in the world were you thinking?

People deal with grief in different ways. I cried and prayed many nights asking God, "Where did I go wrong? When did

I lose focus?" I NEVER gave up on you. I am thankful for our relationship. I heard it said many times: TURN IT OVER TO JESUS AND HE WILL WORK IT OUT. Today, I can testify that I believe it.

Ron, you still had to get away. That's when you joined the Army and left me. It felt like another death, but I understood. Today, I am thankful that you did. WHAT A CHANGE! Do you remember telling me about all those times you and Rev. (Fred) talked to me, over and over about the same thing? I was listening. I know you didn't think so, but I was listening and I am so glad you all didn't give up on me. I am so proud of you for the change that you allowed God to make in your life. We will always be a team. Remember, "If you abide in Him, He will abide in you." Hugs & Kisses!

I love you,
Your Mother (Mary Conley)

# REFLECTIONS

*"Who takes a child by the hand, takes the mother by the heart."*

~German Proverb

# Writing Letters To Your Son

When a parent writes a letter to a child, it's magical. Consider writing to each of your sons at least once a year, perhaps on their 12th, 18th, 25th or older, birthdays or around the holidays. This type of tradition is a tangible expression of your love and pride, as well as the ongoing hopes and dreams you have for their future. I think all sons and even all children need to be affirmed by their parents or the people that care about them. It puts them on the right road and lets them know if no one else cares, their mother does. When you birth a child, it is a gift from God. When you receive a gift, you should take care of it and hold it with love and care.

Not sure how to get started? Here's one word to get you started when you write a letter to a child: *Love.*

Of course, you want to tell your child how you feel! Even if "I love you" is something you say every day, the message is conveyed differently when the words are shared in writing. For example, you might say:

> *"It's hard for me to describe how much I love you!"*

> *"Being your parent has been one of the greatest gifts in my life."*

*"There's nothing that could ever change how I feel about you."*

*"There have been many great men in this world and you will be one of them as well."*

# Reflections from Mothers

**Crystal Archie**—One thing I'm glad I did for my sons when they were young . . . . Teach them the Word of God and speak it over them in everything they do. I pray that my sons love the Lord with all their heart, with all their soul, and with their entire mind, and that they will always know who they are in Christ. Hmmm . . . . regrets? I honestly don't think I have any.

**Ginger Shrum McClendon**—One thing that I am glad I did for my sons when they were young is that I took them to church, even though I had to do it alone. (Also, I always encouraged them to read.) I've always prayed for God to be most important in their lives, that they would always be kind to others, and that they would be happy and strong in their faith. As for having any regrets . . . I have NO REGRETS at all! I'm proud of my well-rounded boys and the gentle giants they have become. I'm happy God blessed me with BOYS!

**Diane Benz**—I tried to never miss anything they were in at school, sports or church. I prayed for their salvation, a godly wife, and their purity. I think I can say I have no regrets. With the Lord's help, I did the best at the time with what I knew to do. I loved being a mom with two special boys that God had given to me. I am so blessed to have such wonderful boys.

**Delores Matthews**—I have no regrets. The one thing I pray for my sons is for them to know God first, for them to have good health, and to be successful in life. I am glad that I took them to church at an early age, tried my best to teach them right from wrong, and to respect their elders.

**Deborah Murrell**—The one thing we did that made all the difference in our sons' lives was to teach them to love Jesus, and we are so glad. Since they were born, we prayed for the girls that they would marry one day. We prayed that they would meet each other, fall in love, and marry in the right time and season of their lives. No major regrets. The years went by so fast. We made it a practice to enjoy every season, every age, and we did, but you always wish you could make time stand still so that you can savor the moments a little bit longer.

**Carol Fidler**—I'm glad I spent a lot of time with them; I remember thinking of Psalm 90:12: *"Teach me to number our days, that we may gain a heart of wisdom."* We had a good relationship through the years and I'm so thankful for that. I pray for my boys that their hearts would be captured by God, that His plan for their lives would be accomplished, and that they would be blessed with godly wives.

**Rhonda Jackson Kemp**—First off, parenting boys, I feel, is a sacred privilege that I truly believe God has entrusted us with . . . . I don't take it lightly, and I know that He has called me to this journey because He knows that, with Him, I am up to the task. I feel like two of my three boys are practically "raised," although I know I'll always be parenting them. When my boys were young, a wise old lady told me, "Honey, the days will be long, but just remember, the days are short." I would remind myself of that when I was at my wit's end . . . and sure enough, in the blink of an eye, my first two boys were grown and off to college. So, savoring the sweet moments together, and cherishing our time was always so important. Anyway . . . as to the "one thing I'm glad I did for my boys when they were young" question . . . . I'm not sure if you're looking for a spiritual sort of thing, or just *one* thing . . . but a couple things we did early on that were wise decisions was to intentionally put great men of God in their lives . . . spiritual mentors to model what it looked like to love God and love others with a great passion. Some of these men have been coaches, teachers, camp counselors, or just great friends of ours. In addition to the mentors, we simply taught them to love God's Word. I remember taking them with me to Bible study fellowship when they were ages two through six, where they were prayed over and taught the same lessons that we were studying. They would memorize scripture, and we'd always tell them how important it was to have God's Word hidden in their hearts. I remember paying, (yes, paying) them as young tweens, to memorize scripture. I thought, "Regardless of their motive here, God's Word is still alive and active, and even if they are memorizing it with the motive of the monetary reward, it is still a transforming Word being tucked away in their hearts!" So, I'd give them long passages, they'd memorize them, and I'd gladly pay them. It turned out to be the wisest investment we've ever made into their spiritual lives!

I wish you could've sat here on my bed the other night and listened to my 22 year old first-born talk about his burdened heart for a couple of his friends on his track team at Samford, and how he's been meeting with and praying over these guys. These guys are so hungry for some authentic truth and so sick of "religious" people . . . and in Tyler, they've found exactly that. They know that he really knows the Word, and knows his Jesus . . . and they just want to spend time with him because it's all over him. He's ready and able to give an apt answer to their many questions, because that Word is deeply established in his own heart. I am so grateful for the many years of impressing upon them a love of God's holy Word.

As for something we prayed for them . . . Well, this is funny, but I always prayed for them to live lives of transparency . . . that their sin would never be hidden . . . and that God would reveal to their hearts, and to US, whenever they so much as raised a foot to step off the straight and narrow. Boy, did He ever answer that prayer! My boys would get busted for the slightest indiscretions the MOMENT they'd make them! Haha! And they knew that I prayed this for them . . . and they knew their sin would always be exposed. Today, they know that the chastening they've experienced from God was His loving gift . . . and that it's been His grace that has kept them on that straight and narrow.

As for regrets . . . Oh, Lordy . . . I have many! One would be making their lives a bit too easy. They've been given the moon, and I worry that they may be in for a shocker once they're out in the real world. Growing up with next to nothing myself, I've wanted my own kids to have all the things that I longed for when I was young . . . and with the blessings we have, I've probably showered them with a bit much. I will say, however, that they in no way feel entitled. They realize that they're privileged and blessed because of their hard-working dad and because God has chosen to give them much.

Another thing that has proven to be wise for us in parenting . . . is hearing a Bible teacher teach about parenting kids and keeping "relationship" first and foremost when choosing your battles with your kids. I have always remembered that . . . and I feel like we've really gotten that right. We have always kept the relationship in the forefront of our minds when disciplining them . . . and somehow, we've gotten it right . . . and so our relationship with them is strong. Somehow, they think we're cool and fun, and love to bring all their buddies over to hang out with US! We've somehow been able to manage their "disciplining/consequences" in such a loving way that our relationship has remained intact and strong . . . . and we know that this has been key to the remarkable young men they're turning out to be. They've witnessed way too much from their peers who've gotten so far off into sin, that they know it could've happened to them, had they not had parents praying that their sins would never be hidden.

I'm really proud (in a humble way) of my boys. I realize that they are a work in progress . . . aren't we all?! My youngest is fifteen and he's smack dab in the middle of that funky age, so he isn't the funniest right now . . . but like his brothers, I know he'll come out of it. But my kids know Jesus . . . and they know His Word . . . and they are freed-up worshippers . . . and it blesses this mama's heart to see their love for Him, and consequently their love for others . . . and their tender and compassionate hearts for hurting people. I know that most kids their ages are so self-consumed that they don't even realize anything else is going on around them, but themselves. But, I can truly say that my boys have hearts that are tender toward hurting people, and respond in so many loving ways.

# *Advice from Mothers*

When your son was born, neither the doctors nor your mother gave you a rulebook. We learned new things daily as our sons grew and matured. I remember looking at Roland when I brought him home and saying, "Lord, I need your HELP!" I had worked with children for many years, but when it is your own, it is a different story. I have a few tips to share that worked for me and for other mothers that I spent time with.

Teach him how to do laundry, load the dishwasher, and iron a shirt. He may not always choose to do it, but someday his wife will thank you. Make sure he has examples of good men who are powerful because of their character, brains, determination, integrity and their faith . . . examples of strong men that are not just muscle strong but intelligent, great in business, have strong character, morals, is a great friend, compassionate, and don't mind shedding a tear when they are sad. Men like Albert Einstein, Dr. Martin Luther King, Jr., Bill Gates, Colin Powell, Billy Graham, Jackie Robinson, Nelson Mandela, Abraham Lincoln, Richard Branson, Dan Cathy, James Cash Penney, Bishop TD Jakes, Sam Walton, Bishop Rice Broocks, Pastor James Lowe, Bruce Fidler, Pastor Tim Johnson, and Darrell Green are some incredible examples!

We should also share great women role models with our sons. They need to know this as well since they may one day have a sister, a female teacher or boss, or a wife. They will most likely know the well-known celebrity women in entertainment and music but make sure they also know female business leaders, and those that have made great contributions to our society. Women like Margaret Thatcher, CeCe Winans, Eleanor Roosevelt, Maya Angelou, Oprah Winfrey, Ameila Earhart, Sarah Boone, Madame CJ Walker, Ellen Johnson-Sirleaf, Jessica Alba, Jill Becker, Andrea Jung, Debbie Winans-Lowe, Serita Jakes, Mother Teresa, Michelle Obama, Laura Bush, and Rosa Parks are some examples, but don't forget to add *yourself!*

Let him lose because he will learn that he is not always a winner. Even if you want to say, "You're a winner because you tried," don't. He doesn't feel like a winner; he feels sad and disappointed. I learned this quickly when Roland was playing football. I always wanted to make him feel better after he lost a game. It never worked! He didn't want to hear that it would be better next time; all he cared about was how he felt at that moment. This practice will do him good later when he loses again. Instead make sure he understands that sometimes you win, and sometimes you lose, but that doesn't mean you ever give up.

Give him opportunities to help others. There is a big difference in giving someone the opportunity to help and forcing someone to help. I remember taking Roland out to volunteer when he was as young as five. He would go with me to the community events and serve right alongside me. When he got older, it became what he just did naturally. I didn't know he was volunteering at Williamson County United Way until I saw a picture of him with children. Giving them opportunity allows them to feel happiness when serving. Once they participate, they are excited and want more opportunities. Be an example of helping others in your own actions, in the way your family helps each other, and helping others together.

The most important thing is spending quality time with them to hear their hearts and direct them by the Holy Spirit on what to do. It is important to make time with them even if you feel like you have no time. There are things you have to balance out to make this happen, such as work or other events you have on your agenda. When it come to today's type of busy world, social activities and household chores can damage the relationship with your child if no time is taken out for them because of the busyness of our lives. Mine was working all the time, three jobs to be exact. I believe that the time spent with them opens doors for them to communicate with you on whatever subject or issue that concerns them. ~Regina Conley-Hockett

I'd suggest serving with your son through volunteerism. I believe it gives him an empathetic spirit, acknowledges that he can always do something meaningful, and teaches him an appreciation for the many blessings he's received, as well as his responsibility for paying it forward. It's a beautiful thing to see a man giving to others with no expectation of receiving. Praying with him is a given. ~Dawana Wade

One important thing I've done with my son is to help him learn how to treat young ladies and to honor them. He is at the awkward age of eight years old now, and with two sisters, the battle is to get a burp-free dinner! He is learning slowly to respect his sisters, defend them, and honor them. He loves spending time with them and I often overhear him "teaching" his little sister things he has learned at school.

One day recently, we told my son that he was going to be taking Mom out for a mother-son date and that he would be paying! After letting him sweat it for a few minutes, my husband told him he would give him some money to pay the bill! I ended up going in to have lunch with him at school. The expression of joy on his face was priceless when he entered his lunch number to "buy" my lunch! You cannot start too early teaching your son how to respect and honor women in their life, even if those women are their sisters, mother or cousins. ~Cristy Robinson

The most important thing I have done in raising my two sons since they were five and six years old on how to be strong men of God is to talk with them consistently about how to hear God, how to acknowledge the promptings of the Holy Spirit, and how to be led by His peace. Now as teens, I ask them often how God is leading them in certain situations and what they are hearing from HIM. I feel that my job as their mother is to teach them the Word of God, encourage them to seek Him in every area of their life, help them discern His will through His Word and support their decisions. It was vitally important to me to teach my sons to rely first on God, then on me. ~Tracie Bonds

When raising them, have your ears and eyes open to what speaks love to them. It may not always be the way you want to give it. With one of my sons, it was obvious and easy. The other was a bit more reserved, and I had to learn that my giving hugs and saying, "I love you" or giving an encouraging word wasn't really speaking to him. I had to learn to wrestle, scratch his back while he lay in bed, and throw a ball every now and then to connect. ~Shelley McCraw

It is so important to teach your son to memorize scripture when he is young. Kids will naturally memorize songs and movie lines, but God's Word is so much more important. A friend gave us a decorated shoe box with Bible verses in it on index cards when he was young and it made such an impact. He would pull a scripture out to memorize before going to bed and quote it to me. Now that he is twenty-one, I can be confident that the Holy Spirit will bring God's Word that has been planted in his heart to his remembrance wherever he goes. ~Shelia Patterson

While many young men are encouraged to pursue athletics, I have found it great to expose my son to the arts. He and his dad watch endless sporting events, but I have truly loved taking him to concerts, plays, and the opera starting at a very young age. In addition, encouraging him in praise and worship, as well as scripture memorization through song as a toddler, has given him the freedom to worship God publicly and privately now as a teen. He is perfectly comfortable now with his hands on a basketball or tennis racket or lifted up to the Lord. ~Lisa Waters

We pray with and for Jackson every single night before he goes to sleep. We do what my dad calls "preach praying" where we speak/pray things over him that we want to see God do in and through him. We pray that he would "love, serve and follow God all the days of his life," every single night. We also thank God for all the qualities in him that really we are hoping to see in him, for example: "Thank You, Lord, for making Jackson brave, courageous, and obedient to You." ~Elizabeth Claybaker

I think our sons need daily encouragement (Hebrews 3:13a), and that takes time. I was my son's cheerleader. When he was in little league baseball, soccer and then tennis, I was there. I home-schooled and there were academic challenges for my son along the way. And as we mothers know, athletics and schooling bring up character issues in our sons . . . and in us! In the midst of those growing up years filled with challenges, discipline, and disappointments, I consistently reminded him that he was destined to be a world-changer; that God had big plans for his life. We must pour on the encouragement daily. ~Sandy Houston

One of the most memorable experiences that I have had with my son was to teach him the details of driving three months before he was to take his exam. Well, for me that had to require patience that I didn't know I had. At first, it was challenging; all kinds of thoughts were coming to my mind and a lot of what ifs. As the months went on, there were a lot of corrects, followed up with praises. As we got closer to the exam, praises began to increase, which allowed his confidence to rise. The day before the test, as he was driving to school, I began to read encouraging scriptures to him in the form of a prayer. As a mother of a seventeen year old son, I do my best to let him know that I believe in him and that he cannot do anything without Jesus Christ being first in his life.

As my son was in the vehicle driving for his driving test, it began to rain very hard. Normally, when it rained like it did, they cancel the exam for another day. Mind you, he never drove in this type of weather condition before. When he returned from his exam, the instructor told my husband, "Your son is good under pressure," shook his hand, and said congratulations. My tip for a mom of a son is to give correction, praise, life application, and wisdom. Give it to them in little bites, not all at once. ~Sa'Mon Smith

I remember Roland telling me that he didn't see me in the stands. I tried to attend all of his games because I knew he would be looking for me. Remember, your son will call you when he is sick. When he really messes up, he will call you. When he is grown and strong and tough and he feels like crying, he will come to you, because a man can cry in front of his mother without feeling self-conscious. The more you help your son realize that there are many options in every situation, the more you increase their potential for satisfaction. Laugh with your children and encourage them to laugh at themselves. People who take themselves very seriously are undoubtedly decreasing their enjoyment in life. A good sense of humor and the ability to make light of life are important ingredients for increasing one's overall enjoyment. ~Yolanda Conley Shields

## Self-Reflection Questions

1.  When was the last time I played with my children?
2.  What have I learned from a child recently?
3.  What time can I set aside this week to play with my child?

## NOTES

# REFLECTIONS

*"A mother's love is patient and forgiving when all others are forsaking, and it never fails or falters, even though the heart is breaking."*

~Helen Steiner Rice

# DEVOTIONAL

*"Search me, O God, and know my heart; test me and know my anxious thoughts. See if there is any offensive way in me, and lead me in the way everlasting."*

~Psalm 139:23-24

The psalmist David penned this intimate, open prayer. Whom do you trust with your every thought, motivation, choice, decision, or action? David laid his life open before God. He wanted God to see him and help him to accurately evaluate his pain and joy, weariness and vitality, selfishness and unselfishness, sin and service. Laying your life open before God makes it possible to move out and raise your sons without fear and guilt. Guilt can keep mothers narrowly focused on the question "What's wrong with me?" and prevents us from becoming effective agents of personal and social change.

~Harriet Lerner, *The Mother Dance*

**DEVOTIONAL**

As you think about laying your life bare before God, what do you fear?

Do you believe that God can lovingly handle all that goes on in your mind and heart?

Reflect on your answer and make some notes below.

When you don't believe God can be trusted, you become defensive, deny your harmful or hurtful ways, and deflect any hope of change. When you believe that God loves you and longs to forgive you and have an intimate relationship with you, you can look courageously at your life and change can become possible. Honestly ask yourself, "Do I want to defend myself, or am I willing to open my heart to God's gaze?" "Do I want to deny any hurt or harm I may have caused, or will I allow God to evaluate my actions, reveal their consequences, and offer forgiveness?" "Do I blame others or the circumstances, or can I ask God to unveil my responsibility?" Your ability to examine yourself accurately is wholly dependent on what you believe about God's love and forgiveness. Recall a time when your young child made a foolish or willful mistake. What did you feel for your child?

> *"Never was a mother so blind to the faults of her child as our Lord is toward ours."*
>
> ~Daniel Considine, from the book
> *Confidence in God*

Do you believe God to be distant, easily annoyed, indifferent, or angry? Is he always watching you so that he can catch you in your sin and punish you? Do you believe that God is harsher with you than you are with your own child? Pray the words of Psalm 139:23-24, focusing on a God Who is completely loving and completely trustworthy. Can you bare your heart before Him? Can you be honest? Now write out the prayer of Psalm 139 in your own words, and use it throughout the week in your prayer times.

> *"Search me, O God, and know my heart; try me, and know my anxieties; and see if there is any wicked way in me, and lead me in the way everlasting."*
>
> ~Psalm 139:23-24 (NKJV)

# REFLECTIONS

*"What the child says, he has heard at home."*
~African Proverb

## DEVOTIONAL—GIFT FROM GOD

*"Every good and perfect gift is from above, and cometh down from the Father of lights . . ."*

~James 1:17

Ashamed, worried, and in desperate need of someone to just understand were the thoughts and feelings I experienced when I found out I was pregnant for a second time when my first child had just turned one. Being placed on bed rest and then delivering a 3 pound, 11 ounce baby boy early made me fall to my knees and pray that God would have mercy on me for not appreciating the gift He had placed in my womb. God told us to name him Nathan Chad, and later I came to realize His instruction.

After a long hospital stay, battling reflux and the whooping cough, I watched this frail little soul fight for life and I often felt as if God was going to take His gift back from me. But what a mighty, awesome and powerful God we serve! Against all of the enemy's attempts and attacks, my son beat the odds of man and statistics. You see, the name Nathan means "gift of God" or "God given," and Chad means "brave warrior" or "battle." Only God knows the journey that lies ahead and we have to be obedient to His guidance. Today, Nathan is an intelligent, determined, athletic young warrior of God.

Always trust in the Lord despite the circumstances surrounding the situation and know that God is a miraculous Healer and Provider for His children. God will calm your deepest fears, answer your seemingly impossible prayers, and show up for you greater and bigger than you could ever imagine! ~Carnethia Wright

# REFLECTIONS

*"Children are the sum of what mothers contribute to their lives."*

~Unknown

## DEVOTIONAL—God's Plan

> *"For I know the plans I have for you," declares the Lord,*
> *"plans to prosper you and not to harm you, plans to give*
> *you hope and a future."*
>
> ~Jeremiah 29:11
>
> (Also refer to Psalm 139:1-18.)

It is both amazing and comforting to know that God *knows* the plans He has for us. The Bible doesn't say God "suspects" the plans for us, or that He "might think" about the plans for us. He emphatically KNOWS the plans He has for us. As mothers, especially those that are single mothers of boys, we have cried out for direction, wisdom and grace to raise these "blessings." Many times, we don't know the next step to take . . . whether it be in helping to teach him how to select the right type of friends, or that there are "real" consequences if they make bad choices, or maybe it's teaching them how to have a relationship with a young lady that honors God and respects and values the God in her. He knows the cares and concerns we have for our sons and their development into godly, responsible men of character. After all, He entrusted us, as mothers, to play a vital role of helping with this development here on earth.

In Psalm 139, it says that the Lord has searched us and knows us; that He knows our sitting down and standing up; that He understands our thoughts. God not only knows everything we think about or that concerns us, He has a plan, a good plan for us; one that ensures a good future for us and ALL that concerns us. So, trust Him. Even though we do not know the specific plan for this time in our lives, God does . . . and it's good!!

~Carolyn Parris Foster

# REFLECTIONS

Perseverance—*"And let us not lose heart in doing good, for in due time we shall reap if we do not grow weary."*

~Galatians 6:9

## DEVOTIONAL—Gift From God

*"As for God, his way is perfect: the word of the Lord if flawless. He is a shield for all who take refuge in him."*
                                        ~Psalm 18:30

On a rainy Monday morning in September, my husband and I were piling our three children into our SUV on our way to urgent care. A few days earlier, my oldest, who just turned two, stuck his finger in the small holes on the shower drain and got it stuck. When my husband tried to gently coax it out, it got stuck the more. My son was getting increasingly agitated realizing that what he thought was a good idea, was quickly going wrong. After briefly contemplating a few different solutions to free our son's finger, my husband made a quick decision. And just as sheer panic began to set in my son's face, my husband gave the finger a good yank. His finger came out, but he left behind quite a bit of skin and blood was EVERYWHERE! By Monday morning when we changed the bandages, it was still bleeding heavily and his doctor recommended that we go to urgent care as the wound probably needed stitches.

On the way, I began to ruminate on just HOW MANY similar trips we had taken. Thanks to his love of jumping off of things and climbing from here to there, at barely two years of age, my son had been to urgent care three times. Once because he fell and bit through his lip, once he fell head first off of a bar stool, and now this latest incident. His "non-urgent care" injuries were almost innumerable! He fell down the stairs twice, lost a big toe nail after a suspicious stubbing accident, he's had more goose eggs than I can recall, a few busted lips, and his knees are so scratched up it looks like he's been scurrying around in fox holes with soldiers.

As the reality of ALL of his injuries set in, I become disappointed with my job as a mother, saying things like, "How can you consider yourself a good, attentive, involved parent and have a child who gets hurt SO much on YOUR WATCH?" or "You need to do better before something really serious happens!" He's always been adventurous and rarely finds an obstacle he cannot traverse, but this was ridiculous! Fear of what might happen and thoughts of my inability to protect him began to invade my mind. I moped around for hours feeling ill equipped to deal with, let alone parent, an adventure seeking little boy . . . BUT God!! He reminded me that it was HIS job to protect my son; it was MY job to pray! He reminded me that He not only created my son, but did so with a specific purpose; one that may include some adventure, the ability to be resilient, to take a lickin' and keep on tickin', and the ability to be fearless—something that his mom has never been. And He reminded me that He gave ME this boy to parent and that meant that He gave ME everything I needed to do that job well.

With the wisdom of the Holy Spirit, I can allow my son to be who God made him, not to his demise, but to the glory of God! I watch . . . as well as pray, and trust that God has placed a hedge of protection around him! It's a lesson I hope to have perfected before he tells me he wants to play professional football, join the Army, go sky diving, or go minister the Gospel in closed nations or across dangerous terrain! ~Mashon Gray

# REFLECTIONS

*"God could not be everywhere and therefore he made mothers."*

~Jewish Proverb

## DEVOTIONAL—Praying the Word of God

Before my son, Nathan, was born, the Holy Spirit gave me what I like to call his life-long verse. It's rather an unusual one, in my opinion. It's from Psalm 22: 9, 10. "Yet You are He who brought me forth from the womb; You made me trust *when* upon my mother's breasts. Upon You I was cast from birth; You have been my God from my mother's womb." I learned early on in my life the importance of praying the Word of God. The Word of God is His will for us. God promised that if we pray anything according to His will, He hears us (I John 5:14).

Nathan is my youngest child and first son. Before he was born, and all through his life thus far (Nathan is nineteen), I have regularly spoken God's Word over him. I have seen God do amazing things in his life. I have seen answered prayer. I have seen serious dangers averted, and paths that Nathan started to tread as a teenager (that were unrighteous and unwholesome) be redirected for good. If there is anything that I can say that has made all the difference in Nathan's life and our life together, it's regularly speaking God's Word over his life. The above Scripture was constantly prayed, with personalization, along with other verses (for health, healing, direction, God's will, wisdom, choices, relationships, etc). Without fail, supernatural, God-given answers to prayer would break forth.

There are a few topical prayer books available to help, such as Stormie O'Martian's *"Power of a Praying Parent"* and Germaine Copeland's *"Prayers that Avail Much."* I highly recommend making this a practice with your children . . . no matter what age they are now. ~Laurie Mingus

# REFLECTIONS

*"Whoever walks with the wise becomes wise."*
~Proverbs 13:20 (NRSV)

## DEVOTIONAL—No More Guilt

Raising a son felt daunting at first . . . of course raising my daughter felt the same way . . . at first. My mom's advice to me was, "Oh honey, just love 'em and feed 'em and trust God for the rest!" I didn't start out thinking, "I'm going to raise leaders." I didn't start out thinking, "I'm going to be this amazingly strong mom and be an example of how to's." I did start out thinking I knew nothing except to trust God.

I started working full-time on a church staff when Vinnie was nine. He and his sister spent years of Sunday mornings leaving the house at 6:30 and returning by 2 at the earliest. Some mornings were just plain hard and I remember asking God as I was driving, "Why am I doing this, Lord? You have to promise me this will be a blessing for them . . . that this is going to make a good difference in their lives!" Knowing that God had set me in that position in that season of my life gave me peace. It didn't make it easy, but there was grace for that time. My husband and I always believed that in our service, we were sowing not only in our areas of ministry, but in our children's lives as well. That was the faith that bridged those difficult times. That was the faith that kept me from feeling that I couldn't be a good mother and be in the ministry fulltime. Both my son and my daughter know I've made countless mistakes as a mother, and I hope I've said I'm sorry for as many as I was aware of.

I finally realized as they were growing up that I was wired differently from some other moms. Baking and crafting those things you craft and scrapbooking and having the perfectly clean and put together house was just not me. I finally stopped feeling guilty for what and who I wasn't and celebrated who I was. I tried to lean into my strengths as a woman and a mom and did the job the only way I knew how to do it. Raising a godly son was and continues to be the one thing that matters. The best way for me to do that was to obey and fulfill the call on my life. Our lives as parents speak so much louder than our words. I want our son to let nothing stop him or deter him from passionately pursuing what he knows is God's purpose for his life. I pray I have been an example of that.

~Janna Pastin

# REFLECTIONS

*"Build me a son, O Lord, who will be strong enough to know when he is weak, and brave enough to face himself when he is afraid, one who will be proud and unbending in honest defeat, and humble and gentle in victory."*

-Douglas MacArthur

## DEVOTIONAL—A MOTHER'S LOVE

Communication holds the key for a mother and son to bond. Keeping that path open at all times is very important. The people in this world can be hard to get along with. I often told my son when he was very young, born black and male, you automatically have two strikes against you. Rise above and don't allow society to dictate and make choices for you. Often I feel sadness for our black boys in today's society; so many broken homes and single mothers working two jobs to make ends meet. But, I am reminded of how I made it over; it was nothing but the grace of God. You see, I was a divorced mother of one with many, many trials. Ron, my son, was almost three when his father left us. It was for the better. I held on to my belief in Jesus Christ. *"Greater is He that is in me, than he that is in the world."*

As a good mother, we obviously want the best for our sons, and we try to do that. Now, let me tell you, it is impossible to do it alone without the help of the Lord. *"I can do all things through Christ that strengthens me."* Friends and family come and go, but my God said He would never leave me nor forsake me, and He's proven Himself over and over. I had to find time daily to spend with God, and some days I didn't. He continued to be faithful even when I wasn't. ~Mary Conley

# REFLECTIONS

*"My mother was the most beautiful woman I ever saw. All I am I owe to my mother."*

~George Washington

## DEVOTIONAL—Praying God's Best

*". . . . and calleth those things which be not as though they were."*

~Romans 4:17 (KJV)

While raising my children, I always prayed God's best for them. My first born, being my son, would always try to be with the in crowd that did everything contrary to how he was raised. I learned early in my walk with the Lord to plead the blood of Jesus over my children. My son got into some trouble while hanging with his friends at a local grocery store. His friends were taking things from the store without paying and he saw them get away with it, so he tried it and got caught. I told him because he was covered in the blood, he was always going to be exposed in everything that he did out of the will of God.

Soon, I had to ask God to give me a vision for my son. I knew there was a call on his life to minister to God's people. I started calling him a youth pastor. Of course, he didn't like it. He didn't have a vision for himself, so I felt that I needed to. Now he is a mentor to young men in group homes and schools, teaching them the skills of a barber.

In the spiritual world, words are containers of power that can change your life, direct your future, and allow you to get your life in line with God's will! Words can carry God's power to literally heal your body, bring financial blessings to your circumstances, and bring the promises of God's Word into this natural realm to bless you and your family.

My Prayer: Lord, thank You for answering my prayers whenever I make a request in prayer, speaking Your Word and to have faith that it has been given to me, and I will have it. ~Regina Conley Hockett

# REFLECTIONS

*"Children are the sum of what mothers contribute to their lives."*

~Unknown

## DEVOTIONAL—Applaud Him

It is so important for your son to be admired by the girls and respected by all male peers. It certainly is important for him to "shine," be the "Man." Applaud him for all the good effort that he displays in obtaining this position. Remind him as often as possible not to mistake style for substance, or overlook favor while seeking finances, and to never give up a good name seeking anyone's approval. Everything in life flows from the heart (Proverbs 4:21). Your son's heart will direct his mind, and therefore his steps. Teach him to keep his heart upon the Lord; this will direct him to long life, riches, honor, and that "shine" that will be so bright until everyone will surely be drawn to him. How does he keep his heart upon God? Meditate on His Word (day and night). One relevant daily Word from God will carry him far. You and your son together could dwell on a certain significant scripture, write it, sing (Rap) it, read it, talk about it, pray it, and make it a part of his daily life decree. Reiterate often to your son how important it is to maintain a good name. ~Grace Swift

# REFLECTIONS

*"The future destiny of the child is always the work of the mother."*

~Napoleon Bonaparte

# *Prayers*

---

*"The fervent prayers of a righteous man avails much."*

~James 5:17

## DAY 1—Dear Heavenly Father

Dear Heavenly Father,

Thank You for this treasured child of mine. Although You have entrusted him/her to me, I know he belongs to You. Like Hannah offered Samuel, I dedicate my child to You, Lord. I recognize that he is always in Your care.

Help me as a parent, Lord, with my weaknesses and imperfections. Give me strength and godly wisdom to raise this child after Your Holy Word. Please supply what I lack. Keep my child walking on the path that leads to eternal life. Help him to overcome the temptations in this world and the sin that would so easily entangle him.

Dear God, send Your Holy Spirit daily to lead and guide him. Ever assist him to grow in wisdom and stature, in grace and knowledge, in kindness, compassion and love. May he serve You faithfully with his whole heart devoted to You. May he discover the joy of Your presence through daily relationship with Your Son, Jesus.

Help me never to hold onto this child too tightly nor neglect my responsibilities before You as a parent. Lord, let my commitment to raise this child for the glory of Your name cause his life to forever testify of Your faithfulness.

In Jesus' name I pray, amen.

~Unknown

## DAY 2—Letting Go

Dear Jesus,

Please hear my prayer. I go along each day, trying to run my life my own way. I forget to let go and give You control. I wonder why things aren't going the way I want them to go. I forget to stop and ask what You want, Lord. Please help me to give You control, Jesus. I want to follow You. I want what You desire for me.

Help me to realize that when You close one door, You open the one You want me to walk through. Help me also to realize that what *I* desire may not be what is meant for me, or what is best for me. Maybe it will lead me away from what Your great plan is for me.

Lord, let me accept each day as a gift. Let me follow the path *You* choose for me. Help me to be thankful for what You give me and not to worry about my needs. I trust You will take care of all my needs. Remind me that my role is to care for those around me and focus on those who need my help. Help me not to be judgmental, as we are all equal in God's eyes. Help me to see the good in all of Your creations. Let me leave the judging to You, dear Jesus. Instead, I will concentrate on living to please You! Help me, dear Jesus, be who and what *You* want me to be. Give me strength, faith and hope, and most of all, give me guidance each and every day. I let go and give You control.

In Jesus' name I pray, amen.

~Unknown


## DAY 3—Prayer for a Single Mother

Dear God,

She seems to bear the weight of the world on her shoulders, but to carry it more lightly than I think I would. I see her balancing work and home, money and no money, friends who no longer make time to see her, and I send up a prayer for her. Her old friends have moved on with their lives, and in truth, she doesn't have much in common with them anymore. She is lonely, loving God. She would like company, but doesn't want to make time for new relationships because her waking hours are already full: she is a mother. She walks when gas is too expensive for the car and forgoes new clothes so her child can have shoes.

This is not how her life started out, but circumstances changed from her life of privilege to this life she embraces so fully. Her life is difficult and she seems so tired much of the time, but I am inspired by the love she has for her child. Give her the strength to put in long hours each day; the courage to face those who dismiss her with blaming and knowing nods; the ability to maintain her loving life at home; and the deepest knowledge in her heart that You love her.

In Jesus' name I pray, amen.

~Unknown

## DAY 4—A Mother's Prayer

Dear God,

Thank You that You are my strength when I am weary from lack of sleep from caring for this beautiful infant that You have blessed me with. Thank You that You are my patience as I am chasing after my rambunctious two-year-old that I am so grateful for. Thank You that You are my peace as he goes off to kindergarten and I am the one having separation anxiety instead of him. Thank You for Your protection as he goes through the teen years and You shield him from peer pressure, gangs, and the ever present temptations he will face daily.

Now, Lord Jesus, as I release him into the world as a man, I realize that he was only mine to raise for You. I know that You love him more than I ever could and that he is safe in Your daily care. May he remember all the things that we have instilled in him about You. May he always look to You for his strength, patience, peace, and protection, for You are an ever present Help in time of trouble and a Friend that sticks closer than any brother.

In Jesus' name I pray, amen.

~Shelia Patterson

## DAY 5—For Working Mothers

My Loving Creator,

You know how really tired I am. On days when things are really frantic, I consider how You made the world in seven days—and then I try to remember that You aren't asking me to re-create that feat. Please help me to remain a loving mother to my children and to keep some balance in my life. Help me to remember that You are with me in every packed hour of every day. As I am finishing a work project or planning dinner or buying the kids shoes (sometimes all at the same time), help me to remember Your loving care for me and let me sometimes stop for a moment and just wallow in that. Most of all, my caring Father, let me remember to ask for help and to rely on You for strength when I have none left; for patience when mine is so often gone; and for the wisdom and endless well of compassion and love I need in my job as mother.

In Jesus' name I pray, amen.

~Unknown

## DAY 6—Prayer of a Mother Whose Children are No Longer at Home

> *"Remember not the events of the past, the things of long ago consider not; See, I am doing something new! Now it springs forth, do you not perceive it?"*
> ~Isaiah 43:18-19

Loving God,

What is this new thing You are doing in me? My life is and has been so very full. Each day it has been shaped by the miracle of being a mother. For so many years, my every moment was intently set on the world of raising my children. I was so keenly aware that my family was some wondrous way that You and I share our love for each other. You have given me my children and husband as a way of showing me Your great love—and the way I love my family was a response to You. But, Lord, I am lonesome now. I miss my children! They are growing and moving off and they no longer rely on me in the same way. My time is less taken up with them, and at moments I just want to turn back the clock. Help me to see what You have in store for me now. You are doing something new in me. You are preparing me for a new phase, a new service, and a new way of loving You.

~Creighton Ministries

## DAY 7—Prayer While Doing Laundry

I find You so close to me right here, dear Lord. Surrounded by the dirt and scattered clothing of my family, I find this an ideal spot to pray with You. No one comes near here, so it is quiet and it gives me a chance to reflect on the many blessings of my life. As I pick up and sort their clothing, I ask You to give each of them what is needed most in their lives. I fill the washer with my husband's shirts and socks, and ask that You bless him as he wears them to work each day. Give him the grace to see that his work is holy and open his eyes to see the sacredness of each moment of life. As I sort the tiny socks or the overalls of the children, I smile and remember how blessed I am to have them in my life. I sort the larger teenage clothing and wonder at how fast these clothes have become larger sizes—and how quickly children grow up. I ask Your help as I guide them through each new phase of their lives. Give me a love that is endless, a heart that forgives them and the humility to ask for their forgiveness when that is right. Help me keep them from danger, and help me to let go and trust You when it is time to do that. I try so hard to be perfect but lead me to remember that it is here in the smudged, disorganized and disheveled part of life that I find You the nearest. Thank You, dearest Lord, for so much grace in my life!

~Creighton Ministries

# REFLECTIONS

"Grown don't mean nothing to a mother. A child is a child. They get bigger, older, but *grown*? What's that supposed to mean? In my heart, it don't mean a thing."

~Toni Morrison, *Beloved* (1987)

## Prayers Found in the Bible

The Bible tells us that children are a gift from the Lord. These verses and parents' prayers for a child will assist you in reflecting on God's Word and remembering His promises as you dedicate your precious gift back to God in prayer.

~Matthew 6:9-15 (NIV)

*"This, then, is how you should pray:*
*"'Our Father in heaven,*
*hallowed be your name,*
*your kingdom come,*
*your will be done*
*on earth as it is in heaven.*
*Give us today our daily bread.*
*Forgive us our debts,*
*as we also have forgiven our debtors.*
*And lead us not into temptation,*
*but deliver us from the evil one.'*
*For if you forgive men when they sin against you, your heavenly Father*
*will also forgive you. But if you do not forgive men their sins, your*
*Father will not forgive your sins."*

~1 Chronicles 4:10 (NIV)
*"Jabez cried out to the God of Israel, 'Oh, that you would bless me and*
*enlarge my territory! Let your hand be with me, and keep me from*
*harm so that I will be free from pain' And God granted his request."*

~Colossians 1:9-12 (NIV)
*"For this reason, since the day we heard about you, we have not*
*stopped praying for you and asking God to fill you with the knowledge*
*of his will through all spiritual wisdom and understanding. And we*
*pray this in order that you may live a life worthy of the Lord and may*
*please him in every way: bearing fruit in every good work, growing in*
*the knowledge of God, being strengthened with all power according to*

*his glorious might so that you may have great endurance and patience, and joyfully giving thanks to the Father, who has qualified you to share in the inheritance of the saints in the kingdom of light."*

~Ephesians 3:14-21 (NIV)
*"For this reason I kneel before the Father, from whom his whole family in heaven and on earth derives its name. I pray that out of his glorious riches he may strengthen you with power through his Spirit in your inner being, so that Christ may dwell in your hearts through faith. And I pray that you, being rooted and established in love, may have power, together with all the saints, to grasp how wide and long and high and deep is the love of Christ, and to know this love that surpasses knowledge—that you may be filled to the measure of all the fullness of God. Now to him who is able to do immeasurably more than all we ask or imagine, according to his power that is at work within us, to him be glory in the church and in Christ Jesus throughout all generations, forever and ever! Amen."*

~Ephesians 1:15-23 (NLT)
*"Ever since I first heard of your strong faith in the Lord Jesus and your love for God's people everywhere, I have not stopped thanking God for you. I pray for you constantly, asking God, the glorious Father of our Lord Jesus Christ, to give you spiritual wisdom and insight so that you might grow in your knowledge of God. I pray that your hearts will be flooded with light so that you can understand the confident hope he has given to those he called-his holy people who are his rich and glorious inheritance. I also pray that you will understand the incredible greatness of God's power for us who believe him. This is the same mighty power that raised Christ from the dead and seated him in the place of honor at God's right hand in the heavenly realms. Now he is far above any ruler or authority or power or leader or anything else-not only in this world but also in the world to come. God has put all things under the authority of Christ and has made him head over all things for the benefit of the church. And the church is his body; it is made full and complete by Christ, who fills all things everywhere with himself."*

~2 Samuel 7:18-29 (NLT)

*"Then King David went in and sat before the LORD and prayed, "Who am I, O Sovereign LORD, and what is my family, that you have brought me this far? And now, Sovereign LORD, in addition to everything else, you speak of giving me a lasting dynasty! Do you deal with everyone this way, O Sovereign LORD? What more can I say? You know what I am really like, Sovereign LORD. For the sake of your promise and according to your will, you have done all these great things and have shown them to me. "How great you are, O Sovereign LORD! There is no one like you—there is no other God. We have never even heard of another god like you! What other nation on earth is like Israel? What other nation, O God, have you redeemed from slavery to be your own people? You made a great name for yourself when you rescued your people from Egypt. You performed awesome miracles and drove out the nations and gods that stood in their way. You made Israel your people forever, and you, O LORD, became their God. "And now, O LORD God, do as you have promised concerning me and my family. Confirm it as a promise that will last forever. And may your name be honored forever so that all the world will say, 'The LORD Almighty is God over Israel!' And may the dynasty of your servant David be established in your presence. "O LORD Almighty, God of Israel, I have been bold enough to pray this prayer because you have revealed that you will build a house for me—an eternal dynasty! For you are God, O Sovereign LORD. Your words are truth, and you have promised these good things to me, your servant. And now, may it please you to bless me and my family so that our dynasty may continue forever before you. For when you grant a blessing to your servant, O Sovereign LORD, it is an eternal blessing!"*

~ Jude 1:24-25 (NLT)

*"Now all glory to God, who is able to keep you from falling away and will bring you with great joy into his glorious presence without a single fault. All glory to him who alone is God, our Savior through Jesus Christ our Lord. All glory, majesty, power, and authority are his before all time, and in the present, and beyond all time! Amen."*

~1 Samuel 1:26-26 (NIV)
*"[Hannah to the Priest Eli] As surely as you live, my lord, I am the woman who stood here beside you praying to the LORD. I prayed for this child, and the LORD has granted me what I asked of him. So now I give him to the LORD. For his whole life he will be given over to the LORD."*

~Psalm 127:3 (NLT)
*"Children are a gift from the Lord; they are a reward from him."*

~Proverbs 22:6 (NLT)
*"Direct your children onto the right path, and when they are older, they will not leave it."*

## Focused Prayers for Your Sons

1.  **Love**—Grant, Lord, that my son may learn to live a life of love, as he walks with you. (Matthew 7:12; Ephesians 5:2)

2.  **Honesty and Integrity**—God, create a clean heart in my son so that he may walk in integrity and honesty. (Psalm 51:10)

3.  **Self-Control**—Father, help my son to be a leader, not a follower; let him be alert and self-controlled in all he does. (1 Peter 1:5-7)

4.  **Love for God's Word**—May my son grow to find Your Word more precious each day so that he will constantly walk in obedience to it. (1 John 2:5)

5.  **Mercy**—May my son always be merciful, just as his Father is merciful. (Lamentations 3:22-23)

6.  **Faithfulness**—Let love and faithfulness never leave my Son. (1 Corinthians 13:2; 2 Timothy 4:7)

7.  **Courage**—May my son always be strong and courageous in his character and in his actions. (1 Chronicles 28:20)

8.  **Kindness**—Lord, may my son always try to be kind and do acts of kindness. (Ephesians 4:32)

9.  **Generosity**—Lord, help my son be generous and willing to share his time, talent and treasure. (Acts 20:35)

10. **Perseverance**—Lord, teach my son perseverance in all that he does, and help him run the race until the end. (Psalms 27:14)

11. **Humility**—God, please cultivate in my son the ability to show true humility. (Matthew 18:4)

12. **Responsibility**—Grant that my son may learn responsibility, for he who plants and waters receives a return. (1 Corinthians 3:8)

13. **Self-Discipline**—Father, I pray that my son will be temperate and sound in his faith and all that he puts his hand to. (Titus 2:2)

# REFLECTIONS

*"Being a full-time mother is one of the highest salaried jobs . . . since the payment is pure love."*

-Mildred B. Vermont

## Our Children

Who will sing our songs when we are gone?
When we are gone who will sing?
Who will keep our songs from vanishing?
**OUR CHILDREN**
Who will lift each voice and sing out loud?
Who will hold their heads high and stand tall and proud?
**OUR CHILDREN**
Who will learn from lessons that our songs ring true?
**OUR CHILDREN**
Who will clap their hands and pat their feet?
Who will nod their heads to our rhythms beat?
**OUR CHILDREN**
Who will go to the mountain top and tell it from there?
Who will spread our history everywhere?
**OUR CHILDREN**
Who will preserve the chronicles that we have compiled?
Who will never have to feel like a motherless child?

**OUR CHILDREN**
Who will overcome the trails of their day?
Who will triumph above obstacles in their pathway?
**OUR CHILDREN**
Who will trust in their own visions by remembering our past?
When we are gone who will make our songs last?
**OUR CHILDREN**

~Burnece Brunson

## LETTER TO YOUR SON

Dear Kenneth,

The day you were born I knew there was something special about you. Now at 51 years old, to see all that you have accomplished has made me very proud of you: finishing high school and going on to get an established job and retiring after 30 years of labor with the State of Tennessee. This shows that you can accomplish things in life without having degrees, but being diligent in whatever you put your mind to. Your great sense of humor is the joy of our family. Continue to put God first in your life and all that He has for you will come. *"Seek the kingdom of God above all else, and live righteously, and he will give you everything you need."* ~Matthew 12:33 (NLT)

Love you,
Mama (Willodes Conley Thompson)


Dear Robert Parnel Conley (1964-1976),

My baby boy, the thought of losing you was my worse nightmare. I didn't know what to do, where to go, or what to think. How could this have happened to you? You were so young and vibrant, interested in everything, and you had all the life around you and in you. I couldn't help to think of all the love and nurturing that had gone into your young life—caring for you, raising you, nursing you when you were sick and taking you to the doctors when you needed that, teaching you all the things you needed to know to keep you safe in this crazy world and most of all, how to be a great man. It was like a bolt of lightning ripping through my heart when I received the message that my son was dead. It felt like I had been stabbed in the heart with a razor-sharp knife. How could it be that you would die before me? Why you? The pain was unbelievable and unendurable, but endure we did, badly, like zombies, wondering when the pain would subside, how we'd go on living our lives, how would we, how could we, ever be happy again. Your twelve years on this earth were short, but not incomplete. God needed you most.

As I write this letter, I can remember how you would crawl up in my bed at night to sleep with me. I would pick you up and put you back into your own bed and when I'd wake up the next morning, there you would be. You were always such a great helper to our neighbors. I miss the meekness of your character and your soft-spoken voice.

Love you,
Mama (Willodes Conley Thompson)

# REFLECTIONS

*"A boy's best friend is his mother."*
~Joseph Stefano

# REFLECTIONS

*"Youth fades, love droops, the leaves of friendship fall; a mother's secret hope outlives them all."*

-Oliver Wendell Holmes

# Conclusion

As we end this journey together, I hope that you have put some of the things that you read to practice. More than ever before, our sons need us to be present in their lives. As we watch the news and read the paper, we are seeing more troubled boys and men each day. Take time right now to go call your son if he's older and has left home, or spend more time with your son if he is still at home. No matter the age of your sons, they need to be affirmed by their mother and father. Take time now to sit down and write the letter to them letting them know how you feel and how much you love them. It works if they are ten or fifty. There is something about reading a letter from your mother or father. I now understand the relationship my mom had with my little brother. She had a different look on her face when he entered the room. He could ask for anything and get it. My little brother Robert died at the age of twelve, and I think a piece of my mother died with him. I know she loves all of her children, but there is something different about mother-son relationships. I believe part of a mother's bond is the fact that she birthed the child.

Start your journey today writing a letter to your son so that he knows how you feel about him and doesn't have to spend years trying to figure it out. I believe this will help him become a man of great character, a great father and friend.

My prayer for my son is: "Father God, I come to You today to intercede on behalf of my son, and I thank You that he has dedicated himself to serve You all of his healthy, prosperous, victorious life, for it is You Who works in him both to will and do Your good pleasure! I thank You for saving, healing, protecting, loving, forgiving, and delivering him. I thank You for the Holy Spirit, Who daily guides my son and imparts wisdom to him, revealing to him the importance of following Jesus every day of his life, as well as having a personal relationship with Him. I decree that my child is a bold witness for the Lord Jesus Christ (Acts 4:31, 33). I pray that my son always knows where he is supposed to be, and goes there; knows what he's supposed to do and does it; knows who he's supposed to be with or not be with and obeys those promptings, because he's filled with the Holy Spirit and led by the Inward Witness (Romans 8:14-16; 1 John 5:9,10; Proverbs 3:5,6). I pray that every moment of his life, he's at the right place at the right time, and if anyone or anything is in his life that is not of You, Father God, You remove those influences from my son. Thank You, God, for giving him the right friends, the right spouse and the right relationships. In Jesus' name I pray, amen."

# PRAYER JOURNAL

*"When we bring sunshine into the lives of others, we're warmed by it ourselves."*

~Barbara Johnson

# PRAYER JOURNAL

*"God sees us through our Mothers' eyes and rewards us for our virtues."*

~Ganeshan Venkatarman

# PRAYER JOURNAL

"Our only true power is the power of prayer. When we pray, God moves from heaven. When we pray, things happen that would not otherwise happen. By prayer all things are possible."

~Dr. Ray Pritchard

## PRAYER JOURNAL

*"Prayer succeeds when all else fails."*
                                    ~E.M. Bounds

# PRAYER JOURNAL

*"Men ought always to pray, and not faint."*

~Luke 18:1

# PRAYER JOURNAL

*"We have to pray with our eyes on God, not on the difficulties."*

~Oswald Chambers

# PRAYER JOURNAL

"*Pray alone. Let prayer be the key of the morning and the bolt at night. The best way to fight against sin is to fight it on our knees.*"

-Philip Henry

# PRAYER JOURNAL

*"Never say you will pray about a thing; pray about it."*
                                                    ~Oswald Chambers

# PRAYER JOURNAL

*"Be anxious for nothing, but in everything by prayer and supplication, with thanksgiving, let your requests be made known to God."*

~Philippians 4:6

# PRAYER JOURNAL

*"We will find that the more we pray, the more we will find to pray about."*

~Stormie Omartian

# PRAYER JOURNAL

*"Children are a gift from the Lord; they are a reward from him."*

~Psalm 127:3 (NLT)

# PRAYER JOURNAL

*"Direct your children onto the right path, and when they are older, they will not leave it."*

~Proverbs 22:6 (NLT)_

## PRAYER JOURNAL

*Pray regularly.* Bring every concern, dream, and desire about your child to God in fervent, persistent prayer. (Luke 18:1-8 contains a great parable on persistent prayer that must have been for parents of teenagers.)

# PRAYER JOURNAL

*"The heart of a mother is a deep abyss at the bottom of which you will always find forgiveness."*

~Honore' de Balzac

# PRAYER JOURNAL

*"The joys of motherhood are never fully experienced until the children are in bed."*

~Author Unknown

# PRAYER JOURNAL

*"Making the decision to have a child is momentous. It is to decide forever to have your heart go walking around outside your body."*

-Elizabeth Stone

# PRAYER JOURNAL

*"A mother is not a person to lean on, but a person to make leaning unnecessary."*

~Dorothy Canfield Fisher

# PRAYER JOURNAL

*"The prayer of the upright is His delight."*

~Proverbs 15:8

# PRAYER JOURNAL

*"And the prayer of faith will save the sick, and the Lord will raise him up. And if he has committed sins, he will be forgiven."*

-James 5:15 (NKJV)

# PRAYER JOURNAL

*"Prayer is not asking. Prayer is putting oneself in the hands of God, at His disposition, and listening to His voice in the depth of our hearts."*

~Mother Teresa

# Small Group Study—Learning to Let Go When Your Son is Older

> *"Love recognizes no barriers. It jumps hurdles, leaps fences, penetrates walls to arrive at it destination full of hope."*
>
> ~Maya Angelou

## How to Get Started

- Plan a 5 session study
- Pick a facilitator or coach
- Schedule a start date
- Invite those that you would like to attend

## Discussion Questions

1. What is one thing you struggled to let go of when raising your son?
2. How did you move forward after letting go?
3. What did you learn from letting go?
4. If your son is younger, what are your fears?

> *"The Lord will accomplish what concerns me; thy loving-kindness, O Lord, is everlasting; do not forsake the works of thy hands."*
>
> ~Psalm 138:8

## Action Steps

1. Share with your son the concerns you have about letting go.
2. Write your son a letter if you haven't done so already (if too young to read save it until he's older).
3. Write down 5 things that you are praying for your son.

## To Boyce

*I want my son to build a bridge*
*    To span a river wide.*
*I want my son to build a house*
*    Fabulous inside.*
*I want my son to build a road*
*    A highway swift, a street.*
*I want my son to build a boat*
*    A pride for any fleet.*
*I want my son to build a plan*
*    To span the universe.*
*I want my son to build a train*
*    The country side traverse.*
*I want my son to build machines*
*    To draw the plans design.*
*I want my son to write a book*
*    Like masters so refine.*
*I want my son to work with tools*
*    And build or dig a ditch.*

*I want my son to sew a seam*
  *The finest tailor's stitch.*
*I want my son to operate*
  *The human heart and brain.*
*To teach a class in problem solving,*
  *Solutions ascertain.*
*I want my son to sing a song*
  *That touches the hearts of men.*
*I want my son to write a verse,*
  *A poet's specimen,*
*To captivate the wishes of*
  *The things that might have been.*
*I want my son to be a man*
  *A plain and happy soul,*
*To hitch his wagon to his star*
  *And fulfill his life's goal.*

~Burnece Brunson, Nov. 1988
(Age 98 in 2013)

# Time to Write the Letter to Your Son

Do you have a great relationship with your son? If you do, it's a great time to let him know how much you care about him and what gifts and talents you see in him. If you have a strained relationship, it is time to work on reconciling it. Share with him the memories that you have about him during his younger years. If there are things you need to apologize to him about, do it in the letter you are writing. It is never too late and this letter could be the thing that brings you closer together. Believe me, he is waiting on it and may not know how to come to you or share his heart.

If you are reading this book and you don't have a son but have a daughter, niece or nephew, you can do the same for them. The principles and life lessons shared in the book will work for all children. Start today by taking 30 minutes of your time to write your letter.

# Letter To Your Son

# Letter To Your Son

# Letter To Your Son

# Letter To Your Son

# Resources

- *Power of a Praying Parent*—Stormie Omartian
- *Upside-Down Prayers for Parents: Thirty-One Daring Devotions for Entrusting Your Child—and Yourself—to God*—Lisa Tawn Bergen
- *Prayers for Prodigals: 90 Days of Prayer for Your Child*—James Banks
- The Anna E. Casey Foundation
- Center for Disease Control (CDC)
- Strength Finder for Teens
- *The 5 Love Languages of Children*—Gary Chapman
- *Your Child's Strengths: Discover Them, Develop Them, Use Them*—Jenifer Fox
- Search Institute
- Public Broadcasting Station (PBS)

Yolanda Conley Shields, CEO of Let's Go Innovate and Vice President and co-founder of the Adassa Adumori Foundation (USA), which does community development work in the continent of Africa and other Third World countries. She has worked with children and families for over 20 years. She is a much sought after speaker and trainer in the area of education, business development, and social entrepreneurship and has traveled extensively throughout the United States, France and Africa. She has been appointed by Tennessee Governor Bill Haslam to the Labor and Workforce Development Board for the State of Tennessee and Chairs the Continuous Improvement committee. As co-founder and CEO of Lets Go Innovate ™, Yolanda's mission is to maximize productivity, enhance profitability, and strengthen parent's, educator's, corporation's, and entrepreneur's ability to grow or launch new business products or services. She has worked with such celebrities as CeCe Winans, Darrell Green, Art Monk, Tony Boselli, and many others. Yolanda Shields, a tireless and passionate advocate for children, serves on many boards. She hopes this book encourages mothers around the world to write letters of encouragement to their sons, as well as reminds them how important their role is in equipping their sons to become men of character and courage. Yolanda has one birth son, Roland Shields, Jr., and many children she supports on the continent of Africa.

You can reach the author, Yolanda Conley Shields, at

https://twitter.com/YEShields
https://twitter.com/Lettertooursons
https://www.facebook.com/LetterstoOurSons
Email: Yolanda.Shields77@gmail.com